THE NORTH KOREAN CONUNDRUM

George R. Pitman

ISBN 978-1547031207

DS955.5.P17 (2017)
951.9—p17

LCCN: 2017944974

Printed by Create Space

Table of Contents

List of illustrations

Preface

This report is the result of a Model Diplomacy discussion group on the North Korean Nuclear Threat at Asbury Village, a retirement community in Gaithersburg Maryland. Model Diplomacy groups are sponsored by The Council on Foreign Relations. The groups' participants play the roles of the members of the National Security Council and discuss current foreign policy issues. Our group at Asbury Village included a retired State Department economist who served in Sub-Saharan Africa and in South Asia, a retired army officer who fought in the Korean War, a retired science advisor for the strategic arms control negotiations at the US Arms Control and Disarmament Agency and at the State Department, and another retired government economist. In addition to material supplied by the Council on Foreign Relations, our group also consulted the extensive literature concerning North Korea and its conflicts with South Korea, China and the United States. At the end of each of our discussions the group prepared a National Decision Memorandum. Although the group's discussions motivated the author to a further study of the North Korean nuclear threat and its relations with China, South Korea and the United States, the results of this study are the author's own and do not reflect the conclusions of the group.

George R. Pitman
September 20, 2017

Executive Summary

For over seventy years North Korea has been a pariah state that has violated almost every norm of international behavior. Its most egregious crimes are its attempts to acquire nuclear weapons and missile delivery systems. Despite of every effort by the international community to contain these activities, including a series of increasingly sever economic, trade and financial sanctions that were unanimously passed by the UN Security Council, they have had no apparent effect in moderating North Korea's behavior.

Ever since the Korean War, Pyongyang has regarded the United States as an existential threat. During the Korean War, the United States deployed nuclear weapons in Guam, and made practice bombing runs over the Korean Peninsula. President Harry Truman announced in a press conference that the United States planned to use nuclear weapons in the war. From 1958 until 1991, the United States had deployed tactical nuclear weapons in South Korea, and most recently President Trump announced that South Korea is included under the US nuclear umbrella, and has deployed the Theater High Altitude Area Defense (THAAD) missile defense system in South Korea and the US Seventh Fleet in Yokosuka, Japan which includes the USS Ronald Regan carrier strike group.

North Korea has conducted six nuclear weapons tests since October 2006, the last one in September 2017 that had a yield of between 75 and 250 hundred kilotons. North Korea is believed to have an arsenal of between thirty and fifty nuclear weapons, and is estimated to be able to produce enough fissionable material annually for six or seven weapons. North Korea also has an arsenal of short and medium range missiles that may be able to reach as far as the US naval base on Guam. It has put a medium range solid propellant missile, the Pukguksong, into mass production and that has been launched from both a submarine and a ground mobile launcher. It has also claimed to have tested an intercontinental ballistic missile capable of reaching Chicago and Denver. Whether this missile has this operational capability is uncertain, but North Korea can eventually be expected to develop this capability

The United States has tried three times to negotiate with North Korea to eliminate its nuclear weapons and ballistic missile programs. During the 1990s the United States and North Korea negotiated the Framework Agreement; in which North Korea would eliminate its nuclear weapons and missile programs; remain a party to the Nuclear Nonproliferation Treaty (NPT); allow International Atomic Energy Agency inspectors back into North Korea; and initiate steps for the reunification of the two Koreas. In exchange, the United States agreed to provide North Korea with two proliferation proof light water nuclear reactors and a supply of fuel oil while the reactors were under construction; the United States would normalize relations with Pyongyang; and promised it would not attack North Korea. But the agreement fell apart almost immediately after it was signed when Pyongyang disclosed that it was building a uranium enrichment facility, withdrew from the NPT and claimed that it had the inherent right as a sovereign nation to possess nuclear weapons.

The second attempted negotiation was the Six Party Talks that included South Korea, China, Russia, Japan in addition to the United States and North Korea which attempted to reach a comprehensive agreement on a range of issues, but the negotiations collapsed after North Korea conducted its first nuclear test in October 2006 during a recess in the talks. In 2012 Washington and Pyongyang reached the Leap Day Agreement in which the United States would provide North Korea with 240,000 tons of nutritional aid in exchange for North Korea eliminating its nuclear weapons and missile programs. But this agreement collapsed two months later which North Korea launched a missile. China attempted to restart the Six Party Talks in 2013, but North Korea refused.

North Korea's leaders have adopted a political ideology of juche which emphasizes the total self-reliance and independence of North Korea even though North Korea is dependent on China and the international community for ninety percent of its fuel oil and for forty-five percent of its food.

China's relationship with North Korea is a complex one. On the one hand, China has supported international attempts to convince North Korea to eliminate its nuclear weapons and missile programs. It has supported every UN Security Council Resolution that has put an increasingly sever regime of sanctions on North Korea, except for sanctions on subsistence items such as food and fuel oil to prevent the Pyongyang regime from collapsing. China regards North Korea as a buffer between it and South Korea where 28,500 US troops are stationed and where the United States has deployed the THAAD missile defense system. The United States has pledged to defend South Korea if it is attacked and has placed South Korea under its nuclear umbrella.

Any agreement with North Korea would necessarily involve China because Beijing has much more leverage over Pyongyang than Washington does, although recently Pyongyang has accused China of "dancing to the tune of the Americans" after China stopped buying coal.

Since North Korea regards the United States as an existential threat, its two primary strategic objectives are first, its continued existence, and second the reunification of the Korean Peninsula under its rule, and its nuclear weapons serve both purposes. from North Korea.

There are three possible outcomes to the North Korean conundrum: war, a negotiated solution; and a continuation of the cold war status quo. There is universal agreement that a war would be a disaster for all the involved parties. North Korea has deployed its heavy artillery and short range missiles just north of the demilitarized zone that could cause hundreds of thousands of noncombatant deaths in the northern part of South Korea where fifty percent of its population live. A war would involve both China and the United States so that three nuclear powers would be involved, and if North Korea felt it was losing, it might use its nuclear weapons in a last desperate effort even if it knew that it would be annihilated. A war would likely result in a long term hostility between the United States and China and could destroy the relations between the United States and South Korea and Japan. Although Beijing has said that it would not support North Korea if it initiated a war, Kim Song-un may believe that Beijing would not allow his regime to fall because it would mean that South Korea and thousands of US troops on China's border, or that Chinese and North Korean forces would defeat the US and South Korean forces.

Although a negotiated solution is the most desirable outcome it is also the least likely. We have tried three times already and each time Pyongyang has almost immediately violated the agreement causing each to collapse.

The most likely outcome is a continuation of the status quo in which a state of mutual deterrence exists through the threat of mutual assured destruction or MAD which prevailed during the Cold War between the Soviet Union and the west. It is a very robust strategy which requires a minimum of rationality to work because it assures that an aggressor that initiates a war cannot win and would suffer horrendous unacceptable consequences. Yet it would be a continuation of the cold war which Kim Song-un is unlikely to perceive as a satisfactory situation. In the long run, the status quo could be an unstable situation in which Pyongyang, counting on China's support could launch a war.

Acknowledgements

Discussions with the following people contributed greatly to the ideas and conclusions in this report: Bruce Duncombe, Joseph Feinberg, Carl Frandsen, and also to Gene Grumby for his technical assistance. Nevertheless,. the opinions expressed are those of the author alone.

List of Acronyms

DMZ   Demilitarized Zone
DPRK   Democratic Peoples Republic of Korea
HEW   Highly Enriched Uranium
IAEA   International Atomic Agency
ICBM   Intercontinental Ballistic Missile
KEDO   Korean Energy Development Organization
MAD   Mutual Assured Destruction
MRBM   Medium Range Ballistic Missile
MW   Megawatt
NNSC   Neutral Nations Supervisory Commission
NPT   Nuclear Nonproliferation Treaty
ROK   Republic of Korea
SLBM   Submarine Launched Ballistic Missile
SLV   Space Launch Vehicle
SRBM   Short Range Ballistic Missile
TEL   Transporter Erector Launcher
THAAD   Terminal High Altitude Area Defense
UN   Unted Nations
UNSC   United Nations Security Council
WMD   Weapons of Mass Destruction

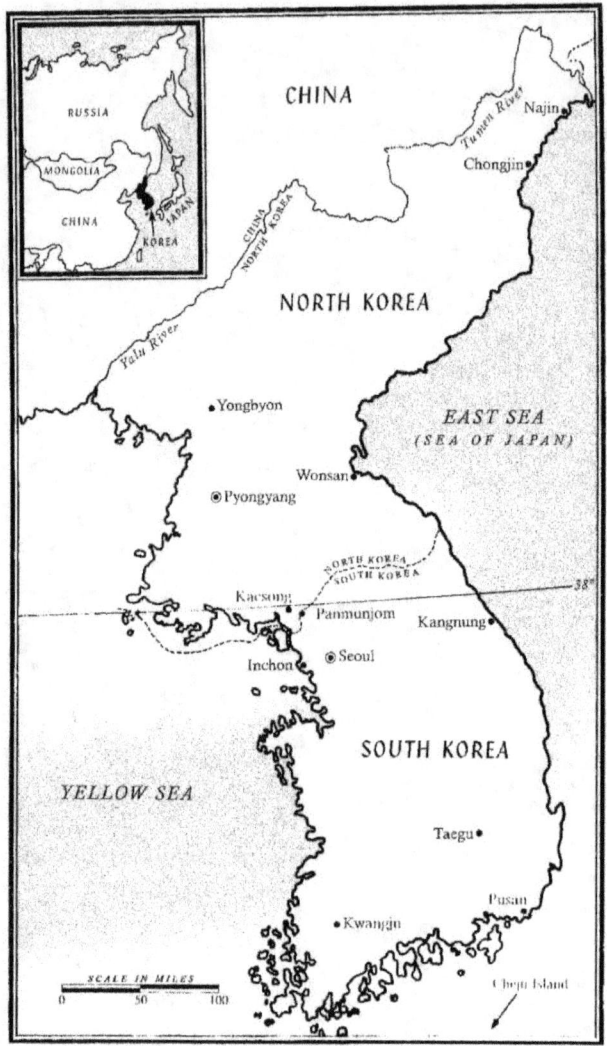

Figure 1 - The Koreas[1]

Chapter I

Introduction

Why is North Korea pursing the development of nuclear weapons and long range ballistic missiles capable of reaching the continental United States? After North Korea's fifth nuclear test in September 2016, North Korea's foreign minister Ri Yong-ho told the United Nations Security Council that his country "had no other choice but to go nuclear [to defend itself] from the constant nuclear threats from the United States. . . . Only a couple of days [after the nuclear test] the United States has again threatened the Democratic Republic of North Korea by flying the B1B strategic bombers over the military demarcation line on the Korean Peninsula and landing in South Korea. . . . We will never remain onlookers at it and the United States will have to face horrendous consequences beyond imagin-ation."[2]

Then on October 19, 2016, the US Secretary of State John Kerry and the US Secretary of Defense Aston Carter met with their South Korean counterparts in Seoul and began discussions on the deployment of US strategic assets in South Korea, including the B1B and B-52 strategic bombers and the Terminal High Altitude Area Defense (THAAD) missile defense system to demonstrate the US commitment to South Korea's defense. In a joint news conference Secretary Kerry said, "I assured the minister of our commitment, the United States commitment to defend South Korea through a robust combined defense posture and through extended deterrence including the US nuclear umbrella, conventional strike and missile defense capabilities. . . . Let me be clear, any attack on the United States or its allies will be defeated and any use of nuclear weapons will be met with an effective and overwhelming response. To that end I'm pleased that we have established this dialogue on extended deterrence."[3]

The first meeting of the Extended Deterrence, Strategy and Consultation Group took pace in Washington on December 19, 2016 and discussed the US commitment to deploy US strategic assets to defend South Korea against a nuclear or conventional attack by North Korea. They also discussed the deployment of the THAAD missile defense system in South Korea. The Consultation Group issued a joint statement which stated, "The US reiterated its iron clad and unwavering commitment to draw on the full range of its military capabilities including the nuclear umbrella, conventional strike and missile defense to provide extended deterrence to the ROK."[4]

During a telephone conversation with South Korea's Acting President Hwang Kyo-ahn on January 28, 2017, President Donald Trump reaffirmed "the US iron-clad commitment to defend South Korea, through the provision of extended deterrence, using the full range of military capabilities."[5] During his visit to South Korea and Japan in February 2017, Secretary of Defense James Mattis again reaffirmed the US commitment to South Korea, "Any attack on the United States or our allies, will be defeated and any use of nuclear weapons would be met with a response that would be effective and overwhelming."[6] In April, President Trump ordered that the Carl Vinson and the Ronald Regan aircraft carrier strike groups deployed off the Korean Peninsula in the Sea of Japan.

On March 6, 2017, the US Army began the deployment of two transporter-erector-launchers (TEL) of the THAAD missile defense system in South Korea. Each TEL carries eight THAAD interceptor missiles. The next day North Korea simultaneously launched four Scud-ER (extended range) missiles as shown in Figure 2 to demonstrate its ability to overwhelm the THAAD missile defense. The North Korean military called the launch a "drill for nuclear war."

The Missiles of August

On July 4, 2017, North Korea launched a two-stage liquid propellant missile—the Kwasong-14—on a highly lofted trajectory so that it would not over-fly Japan. It rose to an altitude of 2,802 km and impacted 933 km from its launch site into the Sea of Japan. Its maximum range was estimated to be 6,700 km, and at that range it could reach as far as Fairbanks Alaska. North Korea launched the missile again on July 28, 2017. This time it reached an altitude of 3,700 km, and its maximum range was estimated to be 10,000 km. At that that it could reach as far as Denver and Chicago. Whether these missiles were tested with the weight of a full operational payload is not known. As the weight of a ballistic missile's payload increases, its range decreases. What the missiles range would be with an operational payload is unknown, but the possibility that the missile could reach the continental United States or even Hawaii alarmed President Trump.

On August 5, 2017, the United States introduced a resolution into the UN Security Council that would ban North Korea's export of coal, iron ore, iron, lead and seafood. Resolution 2371 was passed unanimously by the Security Council. Then on August 8, President Trump told reporters, "North Korea best not make any more threats to the United States. They will be met with fire and fury like the world has never seen."

The following day Pyongyang announced that it would launch four Kwasong-12 intermediate range ballistic missiles at Guam, a US territory in the western Pacific Ocean from which B1B and B-52

Figure 2 – North Korea Multiple
Missile Launches.[7]

strategic bombers operate, threatening "an enveloping fire around Guam." The missiles would fly over Japan and be aimed at targets thirty km (eighteen miles) off Guam. The next day Trump said that his previous statement of "force and fury" may not have been tough enough should North Korea threaten the United States. The next day the president tweeted, "military solutions are fully in place, locked and loaded, should North Korea act unwisely. Hopefully Kim Jong-un will find another path."

That evening President Trump talked by telephone with China's President Xi Jinping, who urged "the relevant sides to avoid words and actions that exacerbate tensions." During the week, US Secretary of State Rex Tillerson had been working at the meeting of the foreign ministers of the Association of Southeast Asian Nations (ASEAN) in Manila to find a diplomatic solution to the crisis.

Then on August 15, Pyongyang announced that it would wait to assess "the foolish and stupid conduct" of the United States before launching the missiles. As the crisis ended, South Korea's President Moon Jae-in made an unusually blunt rebuke of President Trump on South Korea's national television, saying, "It's only South Korea that can decide on a military action on the Korean

Figure 3 – Kim Jong-un Displays a North Korean
Nuclear Weapon.[8]

Peninsula." North Korea never launched the missiles, and the crisis
passed like a summer thunder storm.

North Korea's Nuclear Weapons

North Korea has conducted six nuclear weapons tests since October
2006. Pyongyang claimed that its sixth test on September 3, 2017
was a two stage thermonuclear weapon. Yield esatimates range
from 40 to 240 kilotons (kt), but it is impossible to determine
whether the device was a true thermonuclear device or boosted
fission weapon (see footnote on page 31 for a description of a
boosted weapon). The US Intelligence Community estimated that
North Korea had a stockpile of between thirty and sixty nuclear
weapons in 2017, and that it had successfully miniaturized its
weapons to fit into the warhead of a ballistic missile. North Korea

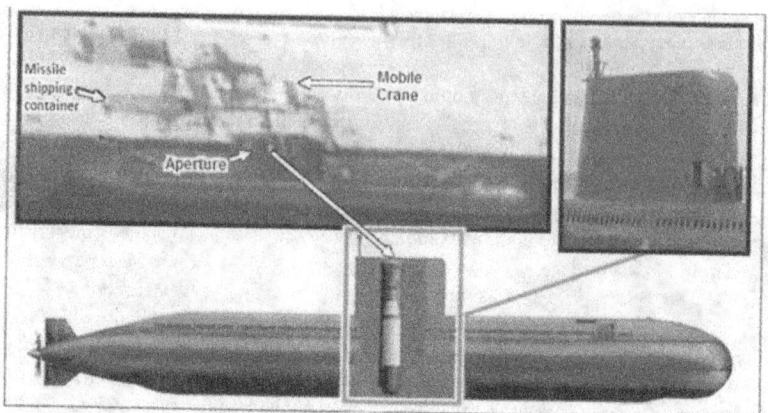

Figure 4 – The North Korean SIMPO Class Submarine with
a Vertical Launch Tube in its Sale[9]

is estimated to have the capability to produce between sixand eight
nuclear weapons annually.

North Korea's Missiles

North Korea has currently deployed between 170 and 200 short and
medium range ballistic missiles with ranges of up to about 1,500
km (930 statute miles). The missiles include: the Kwasong-2, a short
range solid propellant mobile missile with a range of about 110 km,
the Hwasong-6, a variant of the Soviet SCUD-C missile, which is a
single stage liquid propelled mobile missiles with a range of about
500 km; and the Kwasong-7, a variant of the SCUD-ER (Extended
Range), with a range of between 750 and 800 km.

North Korea's most successful missile development is the
Pukguksong missile which has been tested twelve or fourteen times
both as a submarine launched missile and as a mobile land
launched missile. It is a two-=stage solid propellant missile with an
estimated range of between 1,200 and 2,000 km. and is likely to be
deployed on North Korea's new SIMCO submarine which will
have one or two launch tubes in its sale as shown in Figure 4. In
February 2017, the same missile was ejected with compressed gas

Figure 5 – The Launch of the Pukguksong-2 Missile.[10]

from a launch tube that was mounted from a tracked vehicle as shown in Figure 5. In May 2017 Pyongyang announced thatthe Pukguksong was ready for serial production and it may become North Korea's medium range missile.

Pyongyang has also been attempting to develop a long range intercontinental ballistic missile (ICBM) capable of reaching the continental United States. The distance between Pyongyang and Anchorage Alaska is 6,000 km, to Honolulu is 7,400, and to San Francisco is 9,000 km. North Korea has flight tested several two-stage, liquid propellant missiles, but has experienced many failures in its early tests. The two-stage liquid propellant Taepodong-2 missile has been flight-tested four times but the first three tests were failures. The fourth test was used to launch a satellite into orbit on February 7, 2016. It was North Korea's second successful satellite launch. The missile has an estimated range of between 6,000 and

9,000 km which would allow it to reach targets on the west coast of the United States at the longer range. But because of the high failure rat of the tests, the missile is likely to have been abandoned,

On July 4, 2017 and again on July 28, North Korea tested a two-stage liquid propelled ballistic missile—the Kwasong-14—that it claims to be an ICBM capable of reaching as far as Chicago and Denver, but whether it was tested with a payload weighing the same as an operational payload is uncertain. It is also uncertain whether North Korea has mastered the reentry technology that would allow the reentry vehicle to Penetrate the atmosphere without burning up. Several video clips taken from the Japanese island of Hokkaido of the July 28, 2017 test showed the reentry vehicle breaking up into at least three pieces at the end of its fight, but North Korea can be expected to eventually overcome any deficiencies in these systems. The only purpose that a North Korean ICBM could server is to deter a US nuclear attack on North Korea.

North Korea has sold its ballistic missiles, its missile technology and even missile production facilities to Pakistan, Egypt, Libya, Syria, Iran, the United Arab Emigrants and Yemen.

The Military Balance on the Korean Peninsula

North Korea's Armed Forces: Like many other Asian countries, the Korean Peoples Army includes: the Korean People's Army Ground Force; the Korean People's Navy; the Korean People's Air Force; the Korean People's Army Strategic Rocket Force; and the Worker-Peasant Red Guards reserves. The total active duty force includes 1.2 million personnel. The Worker-Peasant Red Guards reserve force includes another 5.9 million personnel. The People's Army is very large for a country of only 25 million people compared with China's armed forces of 2.25 million with a population of 1.37 billion.

The Ground Force includes 950,000 soldiers. It is equipped with 3,500 T-54/55, and T-62 Soviet era main battle tanks, 560 Soviet era medium amphibious tanks, 2,500 armored fighting vehicles, 7,900 Soviet era towed and self-propelled artillery pieces and 2,500 multiple rocket launchers. Two-thirds of the North Korean Army Ground Forces and most of its artillery and rockets are deployed just north of the demilitarized zone that separates North and South Korea.

The Ground Force is augmented with the Strategic Rocket Force. The number of deployed missiles is highly uncertain. One source, Global Security, estimates that only 170 to 200 missiles are operational, down from about 1,000 whereas the Federation of American Scientists estimates that North Korea has deployed more than 500 missiles.[11] The Nuclear Treat Initiative estimates that North Korea has deployed between 175 and 200 Nodong missile whereas the other two sources estimate that fewer than 50 are currently deployed

The Korean People's Navy is a brown water, coastal defense navy that operates within a fifty km coastal exclusion zone. It is divided into east and west coast squadrons. The fleet includes three frigates, twenty Romeo class submarines, a 1,800 ton World War II diesel-electric submarine, forty Sang-O class 300 ton submarines and 10 miniature submarines.

The Korean People's Army Air Force is the second largest component of the Korean People's Army comprising about 110,000 personnel. Its primary missions are the defense of North Korea's airspace which is a legacy of the heavy bombing by the US Air Force during the 1950-1953 Korean War. It also provides air support for the ground forces. Its aircraft inventory consists of about 700 fixed-wing fighter aircraft and 290 helicopters of different, mostly aging and obsolete models of Chinese and Soviet origin.

Given the superiority of both the Chinese People's Army and the US military, the primary mission of the North Korean military is to deter an attack by either South Korea, China or the United States. North Korea is effectively deterred from attacking either

South Korea or Japan because of South Korea's and Japan's defense alliances with the United States.

South Korea's Armed Forces: Although South Korea's armed forces are somewhat smaller than those of North Korea with 625,000 active duty personnel and 3.1 million reservists, it is much better equipped than the North Korean Army. It is the world's twelfth largest military establishment and has an annual budget of US$ 30 billion. The South Korean or ROK Armed Forces are divided into three branches: the ROK Army, the ROK Navy, that includes the ROK Marines, and the ROK Air Force. In recent years the ROK Armed Forces have engaged in humanitarian and disaster relief activities, and in peacekeeping and counter-terrorism missions.

The ROK Army has 495,000 active duty personnel divided into seven corps and 39 divisions. It is equipped with 5,850 modern US tanks and armored vehicles, compared with 3,500 Soviet era Russian tanks in the North's army. The South has slightly more artillery pieces and rocket launchers that the North: 11,300 to 10,000 an it has 7,000 missile defense systems.

The ROK Navy has 70,000 active duty personnel including 29,000 marines. South Korea has a major shipbuilding industry which builds all the Navy's vessels. The Navy's goal is to establish a blue-water navy by 2020. It currently has 110 surface combatants and fifteen submarines. The surface fleet includes twelve destroyers, thirteen frigates and twelve amphibious landing craft.

The ROK Air Force has 450 combat aircraft mostly of US design, and manufacture including 150 F-5, 59 F-15E, 74 F-4D/E Phantom Jets, 118 F-16 fighter aircraft and 4 Boeing 737 Airborne Early Warning and Control (AWACS) aircraft. The force includes 12 Lockheed C-130 and 4 Lockheed C-130J transport aircraft and 75 helicopters.

South Korea also has an indigenous aircraft industry that has produced 20 KAI T-50 light multi-mission aircraft and is now developing KF-X fighter based of the US F-16 fighter and two unmanned aerial vehicles.

,

United States Forces in South Korea: Under their 1953 Mutual Defense Treaty between the United States and the Republic of Korea, the United States stations 28,500 troops in South Korea that currently includes 20,000 in the US Eighth Army and 8,000 in the Seventh Air Force.

In addition to these forces, there are more than 47,000 US military personnel deployed in Japan in the US Navy's Seventh Fleet that includes between sixty and seventy surface vessels, about three hundred aircraft and the Ronald Regan carrier strike group. It also includes the Third Marine Expeditionary Force based in Okinawa, and 130 US Air Force aircraft. The US Air Force uses the Anderson Air Force Base on Guam for staging B-52 and B1B strategic bombers for regular missions over the Korean Peninsula and that regularly land in South Korea.

Joint United States and South Korean Military Exercises: The US and South Korea annually conduct three joint military exercises. The Ulchi-Freedom Guardian exercises are the world's largest computer-=ized command and control exercise. They simulate a South Korean defense against a North Korean attack and include US and South Korean officials and forces. They usually take place in August and September.

The Key Resolve exercises are a two week crisis management and war fighting exercise involving the Combined Forces Command (CFC) of United States and United Nations commands. Some of the US participating forces are drawn from other areas.
The annual Foul Eagle exercises are large scale military field exercises that in 2017 involved 300,000 South Korean troops and 31,600 US troops in March and April and that year they overlapped with the Key Resolve exercise. They simulated a large-scale attack

by the North Korea Army. Although the CFC notified the North Korean authorities of the exercise, Pyongyang complained bitterly that the exercise was a practice for the invasion of North Korea by the United States and South Korea.

China-North Korean Military Relationship

In addition to the US efforts to prevent a war on the Korean Peninsula, China has also been active in preventing a North Korean attack on South Korea. After North Korea tested Pukguksong-2 missile on February 11, 2017, China curtailed its purchase of coal from North Korea for the remainder of 2017. In March 2017 satellite imagery showed that Pyongyang was preparing to conduct a nuclear weapon test on April 15 at its test site at Punggyi-ri, to celebrate the 105th anniversary of the country's founder, Kim Il-sung's, birth. China threatened to cut off North Korea's supply of fuel oil, of which China supplies ninety-five percent, if North Korea conducted another nuclear weapon test. However, after North Korea's sixth nuclear test on September 3, 2017, China agreed to only a thirty percent reduction is North Korea's oil imports.

On two occasions, on May 3, 2015 and again in August 2017, editorials in the Global Times, published by the People's Daily, the official newspaper of the Chinese Communist Party, warned Pyongyang that it would not assist Pyongyang if it initiates a war.

Chapter II

The United States Threat to North Korea

The Koreans

The Korean Peninsula juts out from northeastern Asia and is separated from the mainland by the Yalu and Tumen Rivers. The Yalu runs from northeast to southwest into the Yellow Sea and the Tumen follows a circuitous course from the southeast to the northwest into the Sea of Japan. The peninsula is bounded on the north by China and Russia and is separated from China in the west by the Yellow Sea. In the east, the peninsula is separated from Japan by the 200 kilometer (120 mile) wide Korean Strait.

Radio-carbon dating of hominid bones found on the peninsula indicates that the peninsula may have been settled by humans between forty thousand and thirty thousand years ago. Because of their isolation, these early humans formed a unique ethnic group, called the Joseon or Hangui people, that were the ancestors of today's Korean people. By the fourth century BCE they had been conquered by the Chinese, but by the beginning of the fourth century CE they had gained their independence from China and had remained independent until Japan occupied the peninsula in 1911.

In 676 CE the peninsula was united under the Silla dynasty with the help of China. During the late Silla period Korea became a wealthy and prosperous country. Its capital at Gtongju was the fourth largest city in the world, and the country experienced a golden age of art and culture. It had developed its written language and its theologians became leaders in Chinese Buddhist theology. But by the late ninth century CE, the Silla dynasty fell giving rise the Later Three Kingdom period (892-935 CE).

In 918. the Goryeo dynasty replaced the remains of the Silla. The Goryeo codified the laws and introduced a civil service system that was similar to China's. Buddhism flourished and spread throughout the peninsula. Celedon pottery was introduced and became popular in China and Japan. But Korea was invaded by the Mongols in seven major campaigns from the 1230s until the 1270s. The Goryeo sent its crown prince Chungnyeol (1236 -1308 CE) to the Mongol capital Karakorum where he swore allegiance to Kublai Khan and married one of Kublai Khan's daughters prince. The Goryeo continued to survive as a semiautonomous vassal state under the Mongol Yuan dynasty.

The Mongol Yuan dynasty began to crumble in the 1350s and in 1392, the Korean general Yi Seong-gye staged a coup, overthrowing the Goryeo and established a new Joseon dynasty and moved his capital to Hanyang, the modern-day Seoul. He adopted Confuc-ianism as the country's official ideology. Korea then became a nominal, but independent, tributary state to the Chinese emperor. Nevertheless, its emissaries to China were forced to kowtow to the Chinese emperor.

In the fifteenth and sixteenth centuries Joseon culture flourished with the invention of the first movable type. In 1592 and again in 1597 Japan invaded Korea, pillaging the country's temples and other cultural sites, and taking back to Japan between 100,000 and 200,000 noses cut off from Korean faces. Then taking advantage of Joeson's weakness the Manchu's invaded in 1627 and again in 1637. They then went on to overthrow China's Ming dynasty in 1644 and established the Qing dynasty that ruled China until 1912. The Joseon established good relations with the Qing and experienced nearly two hundred years of peace during which it established a rigid policy of excluding foreigners except for Chinese and allowed a small of Japanese enclave to remain at the southern port of Pusan. Because of its isolation, Korea became known as the "hermit kingdom."

But Korea's isolation ended after China's Opium Wars (1839-1860 CE) and the unequal treaties imposed on China by the western powers in the late--nineteenth century. The western powers, including the United States, sent warships to China, Korea and Japan, and forcibly open them to western trade. In 1882, to protect itself from its neighbors, Korea and the United States signed the Treaty of Amity and Commerce in which the United States promised would provide its "good offices" in the event of an external threat to Korea. It was the first treaty between Korea and a western power. The United States sent Christian missionaries into Korea and many Koreans became Christians.

Beginning in 1871, Japan forced Korea out of China's sphere of influence and after the Sino-Japanese War (1894-1895), the Qing was forced to give up its influence in Korea. In 1897 King Gojong proclaimed the Korean empire and himself as emperor, and from then until 1910 Korea experienced a period of modernization of its military, economy, educational system and its industries.

In 1905 William Howard Taft, the US secretary of war, signed a secret agreement with Japan's foreign minister that recognized Japan's dominate position in Korea; in return, Japan would not challenge the United State's colonial position in the Philippines that it had just won in the Spanish-American War. Korea considered this to be a betrayal of the US commitments under its treaty with the United States.

Japan's Occupation of Korea

In 1905 Japan occupied Korea and then in 1910 Japan forced Korea to sign the Japan-Korea Occupation Treaty, under which the Japanese imposed a brutal and ruthless rule. Seven thousand Korean demonstrators were executed after the reading of a new

Korean constitution and the rise of the March 1 movement in 1919. The Japanese suppressed the Korean language and Koreans were forced to speak Japanese. In 1939 more than five million Koreans were conscripted for forced labor, and tens of thousands of Korean men were conscripted into the Japanese Army. During World War II, the Japanese military forced two hundred thousand Korean and Chinese girls and women to be "comfort women' or prostitutes for Japanese soldiers.

The Division of Korea

During World War II the Soviet Union had not participated in the Pacific theater until after Germany surrendered in May 1945, but on August 9, after the United States had dropped its atomic bombs on Hiroshima and Nagasaki, the Soviet Union declared war on Japan to participate in the post-war settlement in the Pacific theater. Nor had the United States made any plans for Korea in the post-war world as they had for Japan.

Soviet troops first invaded Manchuria and quickly defeated the Japanese troops there, and then they moved into Korea and rapidly pushed the Japanese troops down the Peninsula expecting to occupy the entire peninsula. On August 10, 1945 with Japan now suing for peace, a conference on what to do about the impending surrender of Japan was convened in the Eisenhower Executive Office Building adjacent to the White House. Around midnight two Army Lieutenant Colonels, Dean Rusk, who later became Secretary of State under Presidents Kennedy and Johnson and Charles Bonesteel who later commanded the US Eighth Army in South Korea from 1966 to 1969, were sent into an adjoining room with the task of defining a US occupation zone in Korea. Using a National Geographic map, they drew a line across the peninsula at the 38th parallel that divided the peninsula roughly in half and that put the capital Seoul in the US zone to the south of the 38th parallel as shown in Figure 1 (facing page 1).

Washington asked Moscow to halt its advance at the 38th parallel, which it did despite there were no US troops on the peninsula, leaving the southern half of the peninsula and Seoul to be occupied by the Americans and the northern half of the peninsula to be occupied by the Soviets.[12]

The United States recognized the Republic of Korea (ROK) or South Korea on August 15, 1945 under the leadership of the seventy year old Syngman Rhee who held degrees from George Washington, Harvard and Princeton Universities. In the Soviet zone the Soviets formed the Democratic Peoples Republic of Korea (DPRK) or North Korea and installed the thirty-three year old Kim Il-sung. The Soviets withdrew their troops from Korea in late 1948 and the United States withdrew its troops in June 1949.

Kim Il-sung

Kim Il-sung (April 15, 1912—July 8, 1984) was born Kim Song-un in Pyongyang to Christian parents and was raised as a Presbyterian. He had only eight years of formal education, of which the last two were in Chinese schools in Manchuria that was occupied by the Japanese. At the age of seventeen he was expelled from school for anti-Japanese subversive activities and became the youngest member of an underground Marxist organization for which the Japanese arrested him and he spent several months in jail. At the age of nineteen he joined the Chinese Communist Party and an anti-Japanese guerrilla group and then in 1935 at the age of twenty-three, he joined the Northeast United Anti-Japanese Army (NUAJA), a guerrilla army, .and became the political commissar of the third detachment of the Second Division, a group of about 130 soldiers. That same year he changed his name to Kim Il-sung, meaning, "Kim became the sun."

Two years later, Kim was appointed commander of the Sixth Division of the NUAJA that became known as Kim Il-sung's

Figure 6 – Kim Il-sung.

division. In June 1937, his division captured a small Japanese town just south of the Yalu River and held it for only a few hours. Nevertheless, the action was considered be a great victory for Korea, and the Japanese came to regard Kim as one of the most effective and popular of the Korean leaders. His reward was to become one of the Japanese "most wanted persons" He appeared posters as the Tiger. In February 1940, the Japanese Meada Unit was sent to find and destroy Kim's Division, but instead Kim destroyed the Japanese unit. As a result, Kim was appointed commander of the Second Operational Region of the First Army. By the end of 1940, he was the only one of the First Army's commanders still alive.

Kim and what remained of his army crossed the Amur River into the Soviet Union where he spent the last years of the war in Manchuria, training Korean guerrilla fighters. He was given the rank of major in the Soviet Red Army.

Why Kim was chosen as the leader of North Korea is uncertain. It is rumored that Stalin personally chose Kim and is reputed to have said, "Korea is a young country and needs a young leader." Kim had a reputation of being cordial and comfortable with ordinary people. In his memoires Kim described himself as an ordinary man, and during his 1986 visit to Moscow,

Vadim Medvedev, his escort wrote that "he was greatly surprised [to find Kim as] absolutely normal person with whom he could talk not only about politics but also about the weather, exchange opinions about events happening around and impressions on what we saw."[13] After Kim became the "Great Leader" of North Korea, his government soon became a Stalinist style communist dictatorship. Kim created a cult of personality for himself as so many other absolute leaders have done. He was the country's leading novelist, designer, philosopher and Ping-Pong trainer. North Koreans celebrated his birthday instead of Christmas; he distributed presents to children across the country as Santa Clause does.

He built at least five palaces for himself and isolated himself except for servants, bodyguards, his ministers, generals and carefully screened guests. Special road lanes were reserved for him and when he went out, traffic was barred from the roads he used. When he visited the Soviet Union in 1986, other trains were barred from the rails that his special train used, and when his train stopped, the station platforms were cleared of all others.[14]

The North Korea that Kim created is an absolute state—a true Orwellian state, a religious cult. No criticism or dissent of Kim Il-sung or his teachings wais permitted. Critics were arrested and even sent to the country's extensive gulag even for sitting on a newspaper that contained his photograph. His rule and that of his son and grandson have departed from the traditional communist rule into personality cults.

The Korean War

Kim Il-sung was obsessed with the idea of reuniting the peninsula under his rule. In 1949 and early 1950 Kim implored Stalin and his diplomats to allow him to invade South Korea, and at one point he told the Soviet Ambassador in Pyongyang, "Lately I do not sleep at night, thinking about how to resolve the question of the reunification of the whole country. If the matter of the liberation of the people of the southern portion of Korea and the unification is not drawn out, then I can lose the trust of the people of Korea."[15] Stalin turned Kim's request down twice, but early in 1950 he approved Kim's war plans because of what he said was the "changed international situation." Stalin may have been referring to the exclusion of Korea from the US defense perimeter by Secretary of State Dean Acheson in a speech he gave before the National Press Club in January 1950.[16]

On June 25, 1950 with Stalin's and Mao Zedong's consent, North Korean troops crossed the 38th parallel and invaded South Korea to reunify North and South Korea. The North's troops advanced rapidly down the peninsula until the South Korean Army established a toe hold at Pusan at the southern end of the peninsula.

In Washington, the Truman administration did not anticipate the invasion. It was more concerned about a Soviet invasion of Western Europe, but North Korea's invasion of South Korea alerted it to the possibility of the start a new world war in Asia and Truman's advisors feared that a new war in Asia would marginalize the United Nations and encourage Communist aggression elsewhere. Consequently, on the same day of the invasion, the Truman administration introduced a resolution in the UN Security Council to authorize the use of force to repel the invasion. Because the Soviet Union had been boycotting the Security Council since January 1950, its representative was not present to veto the resolution and the Security Council unanimously approved Security Council Resolution 82 on June 25, 1950. It demanded that North Korea cease its aggression and withdraw its forces back to the 38th parallel. North Korea refused to comply with the resolution and on June 27 the Security Council adopted Resolution 83 that recommended military intervention by the UN member states to restore peace on the Korean Peninsula.

In 1950 the North Korean Army numbered between 150,000 and 200,000 troops armed with Soviet tanks, whereas the South

Korean Army had only 98,000 troops and no armored vehicles. After US troops and those from eighteen other countries began arriving in August, the combined United Nations force rose to 180,000 troops armed with US medium tanks. But the North Korean forces contain the UN forces in the Pusan area until General Douglas MacArthur, commander of the UN forces, landed an amphibious force of 75,000 troops at Inchon just west of Seoul on September 15, 1950. MacArthur's troops recaptured Seoul on September 22, advanced across the peninsula and cut the North Korean Army's supply lines. The UN forces broke through the Pusan perimeter, joined MacArthur's forces and then advanced rapidly up the peninsula to the Yalu River that forms the border between China and North Korea.

Then on October 18 the Chinese Volunteer Army's Thirteenth Army Group—a force of 200,000 troops—secretly crossed the frozen Yalu River at night and launched a counteroffensive against the UN forces. The war became a brutal winter war in which Seoul changed hands four times and then became stalemated along an irregular line a few kilometers north of the 38th parallel as shown in Figure 1 (opposite page 1). During the armistice talks both sides withdrew two kilometers back from the cease-fire line creating a four kilometer wide demilitarized zone (DMZ) that still remains.

The war had claimed almost three million civilian casualties and another five million non-combatant refugees. It claimed 45,000 US military fatalities and 103,000 wounded, and 900,000 Chinese and 520,000 North Korean military casualties.[17] During the war, the US Air Force dropped 635,000 tons of munitions, including 32,577 tons of napalm mostly on North Korea, compared with 503,000 tons dropped on Japan during the entire Second World War. Most of the munitions were dropped on population centers, where an estimated 12 to 15 percent of North Korea's population lived.[18]

The war became an example of a limited war in which neither the United States, China nor Russia expanded the war beyond the

Korean Peninsula. The United States refrained from attacking both Russian and Chinese territories.

The United States Nuclear Treat to North Korea

During President Harry Truman's meeting with his National Security Council (NSC) on the evening of June 25 to discuss the invasion, he asked if American aircraft could destroy Soviet airbases in the Far East. The Air Force Chief of Staff, General Hoyt Vandenberg replied, "It could be done if we used A-bombs." He said that atomic bombs had never been used as a tactical weapon against military targets, but the American military was developing plans for their use in Europe against invading Soviet troops. Truman then ordered that the Air Force draw up plans "to wipe out all Soviet air bases in the Far East."[19]

On November 5 Truman issued orders for the Air Force to develop plans to use atomic weapons against Chinese bases in Manchuria if either the Chinese or North Korean air forces attacked Korea from those bases. Truman then ordered the transfer of nine Mark 4 atomic bombs to the Ninth Bomb Group, and ordered that its B-29 bombers be deployed to Guam.

As the Chinese and North Korean forces pushed the UN forces south from the Yalu River, Truman held a press conference on November 30, 1950. In response to a question about the situation in Korea, Truman put his answer in strategic terms, "This new act of aggression in Korea is only part of a worldwide pattern of danger to all the free nations of the world. It is more necessary than ever before for us to increase at a very rapid rate the combined military strength of the free nations."

In response to a question of whether General Douglas MacArthur, the commander of the UN forces, would be authorized to attack targets in Manchuria, Truman responded, "We will take whatever steps are necessary to meet the military situation just as we always have"

Then a reporter asked, "Will that include the atomic bomb?"

Truman responded, "That includes every weapon that we have."
Question, "Does that mean that there is active consideration of the use of the atomic bomb?"
Truman, "There has always been active consideration of its use."

He then immediately qualified his answer, "I don't want to see it used. It is a terrible weapon, and it should not be used on innocent men, women and children who have nothing whatsoever to do with this military aggression."
Later in the conference, a reporter asked, "Did we understand you clearly that the use of the atomic bomb is under active consideration?"
Truman responded, "Always has been. It's one of our weapons."
Question, "Does that mean, Mr. President, use against military or civilians?"

Truman, "It's a matter that the military people will have to decide. I'm not a military authority that passes on these things."[20] Truman then realized that he had gotten himself into trouble by saying that the decision to use the atomic bomb was up to the military commander, which meant General MacArthur, which made things even worst. After the news conference the White House issued an explanatory statement:

> President wants to make it certain that there is no misunderstanding of his answers to questions at his press conference today about the use of the atomic bomb. Naturally there has been discussion of this subject since the outbreak of hostilities in Korea just as there has been consideration of the use of all military weapons whenever our forces are in combat. Consideration of the use of any weapon is always implicit in the very possession of that weapon. However it should be emphasized The that, by law, only the President can authorize the use of the atomic bomb, and no such authorization has been given. If and when such authorization should be given, the military

commander in the field would have charge of the tactical delivery of the weapon. In brief, this replied to the question at today's press conference does not represent any change in this situation.[21]

After the Chinese deployed new troops on the Chinese-Korean border in January 1951, crews at the Kadena Air Base on Okinawa began assembling atomic bombs but without their nuclear cores, and the Air Force began Operation Hudson Harbor in which B-29 bombers practiced bombing runs from Okinawa to Korea with dummy atomic bombs. Operation Hudson Harbor tested the "actual functioning of all activities which would be involved in an atomic strike, including weapons assembly and testing [of the arming system], loading and ground control of the bomb arming." However, the bombing run data showed that atomic bombs would be no more effective against massed infantry troops than conventional weapons because "the timely identification of large masses of enemy troops was extremely rare."[22]

Later studies showed that although the destructive power of an atomic weapon is many times that of a conventional weapon, their effectiveness against dispersed Chinese and North Korean troops and the relatively primitive nature of north Korea's logistics infrastructure, and the small number of atomic weapons that were available (most were deployed in Europe for use in case of a Soviet invasion), the use of atomic weapons in East Asia was abandoned and the B-29s and their atomic weapons were returned to the United States in June 1951.[23]

The Korean Armistice
Intermittent talks for an armistice began in 1952, first at Kaesong and then moved to the village of Panmunjom just south of the 38th parallel. The main sticking point of the talks became the repatriation of the prisoners of war. Many North Korean prisoners

refused to be repatriated back to North Korea which was unacceptable to both North Korea and China.

After Dwight D. Eisenhower was elected president in November 1952, he visited Korea before his inauguration to assess the situation and how a crease fire could be established. He accepted an Indian proposal and agreed to establish a cease fire line that followed the disposition of the two armies mostly north of the 38th parallel as shown in Figure 1 (facing page 1). The armistice agreement signed on July 27, 1953 included a Neutral Nations Repatriation Commission to be led by the Indian General K.S. Thimayya that would supervise the disposition of those prisoners who refused repatriation to North Korea.

The Neutral Nations Supervisory Commission

The Armistice provided for a Neutral Nations Supervisory Commission (NNSC) to monitor the armistice and to assure that no additional military personnel or weapons were introduced onto the peninsula other than as replacements. The NNSC was to be led by four senior military officers from neutral nations (those that had not participated in the war): two to be selected by the UN Command and two to be selected by the North Korean peoples Army and the Chinese People's Volunteers. The UN Command chose Switzerland and Sweden to provide their two officers, and China and North Korea chose Poland and Czechoslovakia to provide theirs. The NNSC also included twenty inspection teams whose participants would be chosen by the neutral nations.

The United States Deploys Nuclear Weapons in South Korea

During 1957 and 1958 the United States suffered a deep recession. Unemployment rose to 7.5 percent and the gross national product dropped 3.7 percent. The federal budget dropped from a surplus 0.8 percent in 1957 to deficits of 0.6 percent in 1958 and 2.6 percent in 1959. The Eisenhower administration decided that it would have to cut defense spending which meant reducing the US forces deployed abroad and reducing foreign military assistance of which South Korea was a major recipient. President Eisenhower told his National Security Council that the country could no longer afford to station 50,000 troops in South Korea and spend $ 800 million annually to support the South Korea Army. Admiral Arthur Redford, the chairman of the Joint Chiefs of Staff, pointed out that the cost of defending South Korea could only be reduced by deploying nuclear weapons in South Korea. The South Korean Army was more than twice as large as the North's—720,000 troops to 350,000 troops—and better equipped. South Korea was spending more than seventy percent of its national budget on its national defense. When President Rhee was told of the US plans, he strongly objected, arguing that any reduction in the South Korean Army would be unacceptable until Korea was unified. A goal that Rhee believed could only be accomplished by armed force. He demanded that the United States increase the number of its troops deployed in South Korea.[24]

Rhee had been a thorn for the United State throughout the 1950s. The United States was wary of his threats to take unilateral military action against North Korea to unify the peninsula. Rhee was constantly reminded that the United States would not support him if there were any violations of the armistice or any unilateral military operations against either North Korea or China. On at least two occasions the United States formulated plans to dispose of Rhee if he tried to order his troops to attack North Korea in defiance of Washington's warnings.[25]

To compensate for the force reductions in South Korea, the United States developed plans to deploy its tactical nuclear weapons in South Korea, and in December 1956 President Eisenhower approved Radford's recommendation to deploy nuclear weapons in South Korea. But two problems stood in the way: First, the Armistice Agreement that ended the Korean War stipulated that military personnel and weapons could only be introduced into North and South Korea as replacements for those withdrawn or were no longer functional. The second difficulty was the Neutral Nations Supervisory Commission (NNSC) which was established to monitor compliance with the armistice.

By 1956 the NNSC had become moribund. South Korea had become hostile towards its inspectors; and the UN Command and the Swiss and Swedish members of the NNSC had raised objections that there were fewer inspections in North Korea than in South Korea. In March 1955, the South Korean Assembly passed a resolution calling for the expulsion of the NNSC inspectors from the country, and in May the United States decided that the NNSC should be told that their operations in the south imposed a serious disadvantaged on the UN Command's forces and that in the future the UN Command would regard Article 13(d) of the Armistice Agreement that prohibited the introduction of new weapons into Korea inoperative. After discussions within the NNSC and with the Military Armistice Commission the number of inspection teams were reduced by about half. In August 1955 President Rhee demanded that NNSC members leave his country, and then on May 31, 1956 the UN Command also demanded that NNSC inspectors leave South Korea's ports because it believed that North Korea was evading the NNSC inspectors and was importing weapons to rearm. On June 21, 1957, the UN Command informed the North Korean representatives at a meeting of the Military Armistice Commission at Panmunjom that it was no longer bound by Article 13(d) of the Armistice Agreement.[26]

The nuclear weapons began arriving in South Korea in January 1958. Five different weapon systems were deployed: the Honest John surface-to-surface missile system; the Matador cruise missile; atomic demolition land mines (ADMs); the M65 atomic cannon; and the eight inch howitzer. Other systems deployed later were nuclear armed jet fighters, the Davey Crockett and the Sergeant missiles. At its peak in 1972 the US had deployed more than 950 nuclear warheads in South Korea.[27]

The nuclear weapons remained in South Korea for thirty-three years until September 1991 when President George H.W. Bush ordered their removal as part of his Presidential Nuclear Initiative to withdraw all US tactical nuclear weapons from abroad, except for air delivered weapons. The decision was made after consultations in Seoul and after Pyongyang had signed the Nuclear Nonproliferation Treaty in 1985. Shortly thereafter Seoul and Pyongyang signed a joint statement of their commitment to a nuclear-free Korean Peninsula.

The Denuclearization Agreement
After the United States withdrew its nuclear weapons from South Korea, its President Roh Tae Woo announced on December 18, 1991 that his country was free of nuclear weapons, and the two Koreas signed the Joint Declaration on the Denuclearization of the Korean Peninsula. in which the parties agreed that they would "not test, manufacture, produce, receive, possess, store, deploy or use nuclear weapons," and the parties promised not to possess "nuclear reprocessing and uranium enrichment facilities." The declaration also provided for mutual inspections. But the agreement never entered into force because the parties could not agree on how the mutual inspections would be conducted.[28].

Chapter III

North Koreas Response

After President Truman's November 1950 press conference, the deployment of B-29s and atomic bombs to Oakanawa, the practice bombing runs over Korea, and the deployment of US tactical nuclear weapons in South Korea in 1958, Kim Il-sung had good reason to believe that the United States was planning to use its nuclear weapons against his country, and that the United States posed an existential threat to his country. Then when the United Nations command announced that it would no longer observe Article 13(d) of the 1953 Armistice Agreement that prohibited the introduction of new kinds of weapons onto the Korean Peninsula, Pyongyang denounced the statement as an attempt to turn South Korea into an "American base of atomic warfare,"

North Korea's Nuclear Weapons Program
Having felt threatened by United States, Kim Il-sung determined that having his own nuclear weapons was the only way he could assure North Korea's survival and independence, so he asked both the Soviet Union and China for help in developing his own nuclear weapons, but both countries refused him. The Soviets, however, offered to assist North Korea in a peaceful nuclear program and in February 1956 the two countries signed the Charter of the Soviet

Union Joint Institute for Nuclear Research, and North Korean scientists and technicians went to the Soviet Union for training. Then in 1959 the two countries signed an agreement for North Korea's peaceful use of atomic energy that included a provision for the Soviet Union to assist North Korea in constructing a nuclear research facility at Yongbyon, North Korea that included the IRT2000 two megawatt (MW) light water nuclear reactor that is not suitable for producing Pu-239, a fissionable isotope of plutonium that can be fuel for atomic weapons. In 1975 North Korean technicians told the International Atomic Energy Agency (IAEA) inspectors that they had removed only 300 milligrams of Pu-239 from the reactor after ten years of operation.

Construction of the reactor began in 1963 and was completed in 1965. Initially the Soviet Union provided the fuel rods, and in 1974 the Soviets upgraded the reactor from 2 MW to 4 MW by increasing the concentration of the U-235 in the fuel rods from ten percent to thirty-six percent.

Then in the early 1980s North Korea constructed a uranium milling facility to process its domestically mined uranium ore, and a fuel rod fabrication facility. In the late 1980s, the North Koreans upgraded the IRT2000 reactor to 8 MW using its domestically made fuel rods that contained U-235 enriched to 80 percent, which is almost enriched to weapons grade uranium. Pyongyang also began the construction of a 50 MW light water reactor.

In 1980 North Korea began construction of a five MW graphite modulated MAGNOX type nuclear reactor at Yongbyon that can produce Pu-239, and a reprocessing facility to separate the plutonium from the U-238 from which the plutonium is made. The reactor became operational in 1986. Taking account of the time to remove and replace the fuel rods, the reactor can produce between six and eight kilograms of Pu-239 a year. By 2005 North Korea could have produced up to 100 kg of weapons grade Pu-239, enough for between ten and fifteen nuclear weapons.

North Korea then began the construction of a fifty MW reactor of the same type, but construction was terminated in 1994 and the reactor was dismantled in 2010, when plans for the construction of a 200 MW reactor were also cancelled. The five MW reactor can produce between six and eight kilograms of Pu-239 annually, enough for only a single nuclear weapon.

North Korea conducted its first nuclear weapons test on October 9, 2006 in a tunnel in the side of Mount Mantap about 12 kilometers northwest of the town of Punggye-ri in northeast North Korea. Seismic data indicated a yield of only 0.5 kiloton, and vented gasses indicated that it was a plutonium device. North Koreans were expecting a yield of about four kilotons, indicating an unsuccessful test. North Korea's second test took place on May 25, 2009 at the Punggye-ri test site. Seismic data indicated a yield of 2.35 kilotons. Its third test took place on February 12, 2013. Its yield was initially estimated to be 4.9 kilotons, but was later revised to 5.1 kilotons.

Pyongyang claimed that its fourth nuclear test on January 6, 2016 was the test of a thermonuclear device, but US nuclear scientists believe that it was a failed test of a boosted fission weapon. North Korea's sixth nuclear weapons test on September 3, 2017 had a yield of between seventy-five and one hundred kilotons is believed to have been a boosted fission weapon.

During an inspection of North Korea's nuclear facilities by US inspector in October 2002, upon questioning North Korea admitted that it was building a uranium enrichment facility. and claimed that it would only be used to enrich uranium for its light water reactors, and not to enrich the uranium to weapons grade of 80 percent or more. Pyongyang claimed that as a sovereign nation it had the right to possess nuclear weapons for defense purposes.

In January 2017 Siegfried Hecker, a former director of the Los Alamos National Laboratory, who had visited Yongbyon in November 2010 estimated that North Korea had a stockpile of

Figure 7 – North Korea's Thermonuclear Weapon

between 34 and 52 kg of weapons grade Pu-239, enough for between four and six nuclear weapons. North Korea also showed Hecker the uranium enrichment facility that he estimated contained 2,000 Pakistani P-2 type centrifuges, and which satellite photography shows has been doubled since his visit in 2010. Hecker estimates that the current facility can produce 150 kilograms of highly enriched uranium (HEU) annually, roughly enough for Eight to ten nuclear weapons.[29]

On September 3, 2017, North Korea detonated a nuclear device that it claimed to be a two-stage thermonuclear device with a variable yield of from tens to hundreds of kilotons. The initial seismic pulse was of a magnitude of 5.8 or 6.3. It was followed by a secondary pulse of magnitude 4.1 which evidently was due to the collapse of the roof of the tunnel in which the device was detonates. Satellite imagery showed that the top of Mount Mantap in which the device was detonated had collapsed.[30] Preliminary yield estimates range from 40 to 250 kt, but most of the estimates were in the 100 kt range. Yields of 100 or 250 kt could be the result of both a boosted weapon or of a true thermonuclear device. Since there was no venting from the detonation, the nature of the device cannot be determined. Pyongyang released a photograph of Kim Jong-un inspecting what appears to be a two-stage thermonuclear device shown in Figure 7.

Based on Siegfried Hecker's estimate that North Korea had a stockpile of between 32 and 54 kilograms of weapons grade plutonium in 2010, and that it can produce enough U-235 and Pu-239 for six or seven nuclear weapons each year, North Korea could have between 65 and 75 weapons in 2017, and between 85 and 100 weapons by 2020. The US Intelligence Community has estimated that North Korea could have between 50 and 100 weapons by 2020.[31]

Both the US Defense Intelligence Agency and the Japanese Intelligence believe that North Korea has been able to miniaturize its nuclear weapons small enough to fit on its ballistic missiles, and in February 2013, North Korea declared that it had miniaturized a weapon. Figure 3 (page 5) shows Kim Jong-un standing behind what appears to be an implosion type plutonium weapon. Whether this is an actual weapon or a mockup is unknown.[32]

North Korea's Missile Programs

If North Korea is to have nuclear weapons it needs a means of delivering them to their intended targets in South Korea and the United States. In 1965 Kim Il-sung decided that his country should have its own indigenes ballistic missile capability and established a program in missile technology at the Humhung Military Academy, at the Rocket Engine Department at the Korea National Defense College, and missile technology programs at other North Korean colleges and universities. Kim's primary rational for wanting ballistic missiles were: first, the need to deter and possibly defeat the United States in the case of a conflict with the United

States; and second, because of his uncertain relations with the Soviet Union and China.

In the late 1960s North Korea received surface-to-ship missiles and Frog missiles from the Soviet Union and surface-to-air missiles (SAMs) and technical assistance from China to develop its own indigenous programs. In 1977 North Korean engineers participated in a joint program at the Shanghai Academy of Space Technology to develop the DF-61, a medium range, single stage liquid propellant, ballistic missile with a range of 600 km for a payload of 1,000 kg.[33]

North Korea obtained the Soviet Scud B missile from either the Soviet Union in 1976, or more likely from Egypt between 1979 and 1981. North Korea's engineers reversed engineered it for indigenous production. The Scud-B is a single stage, liquid propellant, ballistic missile with a range of between 300 and 330 km. By 1985 North Korea had flight tested and produced the Hwasong-5, an indigenous version of the Scud-B. North Korea began serial production and deployment of the Hwasong-5 in 1985 at a rate of eight to ten missiles per month. About 150 of the Hwasong-5 were deployed, but it has now been taken out of service.[32] In 1985 Pyongyang reached an agreement with Tehran for financial assistance for missile development and production in exchange for Iran's option to purchase North Korean missiles. Iran used North Korea's Hwasong-5 missile in its "war of cities" during the Iran-Iraq War in the 1980s. This enabled Pyongyang to earn hard currency to accelerate its missile programs.[34]

Korea then began the development of the Kwasong-6 based on the Soviet Scud C missile. It is also a single stage liquid propellant missile with a range of about 500 km that became operational in 1989. About 300 of these missiles were initially deployed but it also appears to have been taken out of service. This was followed by the Hwasong-5A based on the Scud-ER (Extended Range) missile which has a range of between 750 and

800 km and became operational in 2003. About 350 of the Hwasong-5A were deployed and some still remain in service and North Korea launched four of them in its March 2017 multiple missile launch shown in Figure 2 (page 3).

Between 1987 and 1989 North Korea began the indigenous development of the Nodong medium rang ballistic missile (MRBM) with a range of 1,100 to 1,500 km. Pyongyang sold these missiles to Libya, Iran and possibly to Syria and Pakistan before North Korea's its first successful flight test in May 1989. Iran and Pakistan conducted successful tests before North Korea did.[35]

North Korea then began the development of the Taepogong-1 which is a three-stage missile using he Nodong as its first stage and a Hwasong-5 or -6 as its upper stage. The Taepodong-1 was tested as a space launch vehicle (SLV) on August 31, 1989, but failed to put its satellite payload into orbit because of the failure of the third stage.

North Korea began the development of a submarine launched ballistic missile (SLBM) in 2011 or 2012 which was designated as the Hwasong-7 or as the Nodong. Beginning in June 2016 North Korea began experimenting with underwater launches of the Nodong and experienced a series of failures and is likely to have abandoned the program. Whether it was ever deployed is uncertain.

In 2003 US satellite imagery revealed a new intermediate range ballistic missile, the Musudan on a launch pad. The Musudan is derived from the Soviet R-27 SLBM, also designated as the SS-N-6 by the US intelligence community, that the Soviets had deployed from the 1960s through the 1980s. It had a range of 2,500 km. After the collapse of the Soviet Union in 1991, some of the Soviet engineers who had worked on the R-27 moved to North Korea where they presumably helped develop the Musudan. North Korea did not begin flight testing the Musudan until 2016 when it was flight tested eight times with only one success compared with

461 successful flight tests by the Soviet Union. Six of the tests were in rapid succession from April to June 2016 which was not enough time between the tests for a detailed analysis of their failures, which suggests that the rapid succession of the tests was politically motivated. Again, whether it was ever deployed is unknown.[36]

The high failure rates that North Korea experienced with the Nodong, Musudan and the Taepodong-1 missiles may have been due to their attempts to use unsymmetrical dimethyl hydrazine (UDMH) as a fuel, which is highly potent, but very toxic and volatile. It is difficult to manufacture and North Korea likely originally obtained from Russia or China, but may have developed its own production facilities.[37]

Because of the difficulties North Korea had with the Nodong, Musudan and Taepodong-1 liquid propellant missiles, probably because of their complexity, in 2012 or 2013 North Korea began the development of a solid propellant SLBM which they designated as the Pukguksong-1 and began flight tests in October 2014. Two of the missiles were successfully launched from submarines in July and August 2016. In February 2017, a two stage version of the missile was launched from a tracked transporter-erector-launcher (TEL). It was ejected from a canister with compressed gas as shown in Figure 5 (page 7). North Korea designated the missile as the Pukguksong-2. Its range is estimated to be between 2,500 and 5,000 km, and Pyongyang announced that it has been put into mass production.[38]

North Korea has launched a prototype of its SIMPO class submarine that appears to have one or two missile launch tube in its sail as shown in Figure 4 (page 6). It is the submarine from which the Pukguksong-1 SLBM was launched. The submarine has a displacement of 2,000 tons with a diesel-electric propulsion system. Its range is estimated to be 2,800 km. The combined range of the missile and submarine is only 4,000 km, not long enough to reach to the continental United States or Hawaii, but could reach the US bases in Guam.

Pyongyang is also attempting to develop a long range inter-continental ballistic missile (ICBM) capable of reaching the continental United States. The distance between Pyongyang and Anchorage Alaska is 6,000 km, to Honolulu is 7,400, and to San Francisco is 9,000 km. North Korea has flight tested the liquid fueled Taepodong-2 ballistic missile four times, but the first three tests were failures. The fourth launch on February 7, 2016 was used to launch the Kwangmyongsong-4 satellite into orbit. When the missile is used as a space launch vehicle (SLV), North Korea designates the Taepodong-2 as the Unha-3. It was North Korea's second successful launch of a satellite and its fourth attempt. The missile's estimated range of between 6,000 and 10,000 km which would allow it to reach targets on the US west coast at the longer range. The missile has not been deployed and may be used only as a SLV.

On December 12, 2012, North Korea launched a satellite using a three stage SLV that it designated as the Unha-9, but has also been designated as the Taepodong-3 ICBM because the same launch vehicle can also used as an ICBM, the major difference is that an ICBM needs a reentry vehicle capable of surviving its reentry through the earth's atmosphere. After the launch of the Taepodog-3 the United States accursed Pyongyang as violating its commitment not to test long range ballistic missiles because it believed that the satellite launch was a missile test disguised as a space launch.

On May 14, 2017 North Korea tested a new two stage, liquid propellant medium range ballistic missile that they designated as the Kwasong-12. It was launched on a steep trajectory and reached an altitude of 2,112 km and impacted into the Sea of Japan 787 km from its launch site. It is the most advanced missile that North Korea has tested and it may become the first stage of an ICBM capable of reaching the continental United States. It was tested on August 28, 2017, flew over Japan and impacted into the Pacific Ocean 2,700 km from its launch site.

Pyongyang announced on July 4, 2017 that it had launched an ICBM—the Kwasong-14—capable of reaching the continental United States. It was launched on a lofted trajectory that reached an altitude of 2,720 km and impacted 933 km from its launch site into the Sea of Japan 29 minutes later. It is estimated to have a maximum range of 6,700 km, about the range from Pyongyang to Fairbanks Alaska. However, it could not reach the lower forty states nor Hawaii. The same missile was launched again on July 28, 2017. This time it reached an altitude of 3,725 km and impacted into the Sea of Japan 998 km from its launch site near the Japanese island of Hokkaido. Several video clips taken from the island show the reentry vehicle breaking up into at least three pieces. The maximum range of this missile would have been about 10,000 km, long enough to reach Chicago and Denver.[39]

The difference in the performance of the missile on the two flights strongly suggests that it was flown with two different payloads. There is an inverse relationship between the range of a ballistic missile and the mass of its payload. As the mass of the payload increases, its range decreases. A detailed study of the missile and the two flights by Theodore Postal at MIT, Markus Schiller and Robert Schneider, based on the known characteristics of the missile such as its size, the flight times of the two stages, the propellant used and other technical features, the payload masses on the to flights were much less than the mass of a nuclear weapon and its reentry vehicle. According to the Postal, Schiller, Schneider paper, the payload of the first flight was between 500 and 600 kg, and the second flight, between 270 and 300 kg both, much less than an operational payload.[40]

Assuming the mass of a small, primitive nuclear weapon is about 500 kg, and the mass of the reentry vehicle including its heat shield is 500 kg, the total mass of the payload would be about 1,000 kg, which according to the study, the range of the Kwasong-14 would be less that 4,000 km.[41] However, if North Korea employed a unconventional highly efficient fuel such as UMDH, the capability of the missile could be much greater than that estimated in the study cited above.

North Korea has not yet developed a true ICBM and the reentry technology that would allow a nuclear warhead to reenter the atmosphere at these ranges without burning up, but eventually North Korea can be expected to achieve this capability. How long it will take is uncertain, but likely within the next two to five years. North Korea most likely preformed the two long range lunches of Taepodong-14 in July 2017 as a deterrent threat to the United States not to attack North Korea.

North Korea has launched its medium range missiles on almost vertical trajectories to simulate the environment of an ICBM reentry vehicle. Although the reentry vehicle can achieve the velocities of an ICBM reentry vehicle, they do not remain in the atmosphere long enough to absorb all the heat that they would on a flatter ICBM reentry trajectory, so North Korea has been observed testing reentry vehicles in the exhaust plume of a medium range missile motor to simulate the time a reentry vehicle would spend during its reentry.

On March 4, 2017 North Korea simultaneously launched four Kwasong-5A (Scud-ER) ballistic missiles shown in Figure 3 (page 5)., Three of which flew about 800 km and impacted in the Sea of Japan. The launches took place the day before the United States began the deployment of the THAAD missile defense system in South Korea. It evidently was a demonstration of North Korea's ability to conduct multiple launches to overcome the THAAD missile defense. The North Korea military called the launches "a drill for nuclear war."

North Korea conducted a massive military parade on April 15, 2017 to commemorate the 105th birthday of its founder Kim Il-sung during which they displayed two massive missile canisters, both large enough to hold an ICBM, but both were closed so there no indication of what was inside either of them. They also displayed the Pukguksong-2 missile on a tracked TEL

The same day of the parade, North Korea attempted to launch a missile from a site near its submarine base at Sinpo on its northeast coast. The missile exploded a few seconds after it was launched. It was the latest failure of a series of attempted missile lunches. The failure may have been due to a cyber attack by the US Cyber Command. Several years earlier, US President Barak Obama authorized the US Cyber Command to attack the North Korean missile launches, but whether any of these failures were due to cyber attacks is unknown.[42]

South Korea's Nuclear Weapons Program
After the Nixon Administration announced its decision to withdraw the US Eighth Army and its 28,000 troops from South Korea in 1971 for deployment to Vietnam, South Korea's President Park Chung-hee initiated Project 890 to develop a nuclear weapon for South Korea. The Korea Atomic Energy Research Institute initiated negotiations to purchase a NRX heavy water research reactor from Canada and a small reprocessing facility from France that would have served as a prototype for a much larger reprocessing facility. A nuclear weapons design project was initiated at the Agency for Defense Development of the Ministry of National Defense that at its peak employed a few dozen PhD physicists. The delivery system was to be a missile based on the US Nike Hercules air defense missile that was deployed in South Korea at the time.[43]

In November 1974, the US embassy in Seoul sent a highly classified intelligence assessment to Washington that South Korea "is proceeding with the initial phases of a nuclear weapons program."[44] The United States tried to pressure France not to deliver a larger reprocessing facility to South Korea, but the French refused give up the potential sale unless the South Koreans government cancelled the sale. Washington then applied enormous pressure on Seoul with incentives including reprocessing under US supervision when plutonium was needed for nonmilitary purposes and tid to get Seoul to sign a formal science and technology agreement. But Seoul resisted, so the US ambassador in Seoul told a senior South Korean official, "the real consideration for South Korea is whether it is prepared to jeopardize the best technology and the largest financial capacity which only the United States could offer, as well as vital partnership with the U.S. , not only in nuclear and scientific areas but in broad political and security areas. . . . [In deciding what to do, the Government of South Korea] had to weigh the advantages of this kind of support and cooperation which the US Government can provide against the French option."[45] Secretary of Defense Donald Rumsfeld told his South Korean counterpart in May 1976, that the United States "will review the entire spectrum of its relations with the Republic of Korea" including security and economic arrangements if Seoul insists on developing nuclear weapons.[46] Faced with such overwhelming pressures, President Park cancelled the French contract and all activities related to Project 890.

But after it signed the NPT in July 1968, South Korean continued to conduct experiments that were forbidden under its Safeguards Agreement with the IAEA. In 1982, scientists at the Korea Atomic Energy Research Institute irradiated four spent fuel rods in a research reactor and then extracted 300 milligrams of plutonium from the spent fuel. South Korea's Ministry of Science and Technology claimed that they wanted to study the chemical properties of the plutonium. Then in 2000, South Korean scientists enriched uranium-235 to 77 percent using laser enrichment technology. At 77 percent U-235 is considered to be weapons grade U-235. During the June 2008 IAEA Board of Governors meeting, a "broader conclusion" was drawn that all nuclear material in South Korea had been placed under safeguards and remained in peaceful nuclear activities.

Opinion polls in South Korea taken over the past several years have consistently shown that South Korean's have doubted the reliability of the US extended nuclear deterrence to defend South Korea with US nuclear weapons if it is attacked by North Korea. Two polls taken in 2013 after North Korea's third nuclear test, showed that two-thirds of the respondents support South Korea having its own nuclear deterrent.[47] Another poll by the Yonhap News Agency taken in August 2016 after North Korea's fourth nuclear weapons test in January 2016 showed that 52.5 percent of the respondents expressed doubts about the reliability of the US extended nuclear deterrent if North Korea attacked South Korea with its nuclear weapons.[48] A fourth poll taken by the Korean Gallop Poll just after North Korea's fifth nuclear test, sixty percent of the respondents supported South Korea's development of its own nuclear weapons.[49]

Chapter IV

The Failure of Diplomacy

The United States has attempted three times to engage North Korea in negotiations in which North Korea would agree to eliminate its nuclear weapons and ballistic missile programs. In two cases Pyongyang violated the agreements within months after they were signed, and in the third case, Pyongyang conducted its first nuclear weapons test during a recess in the negotiations.

The Agreed Framework Agreement[50]
North Korea signed the Nuclear Nonproliferation Treaty (NPT) as a non-nuclear weapons state in December 1985 to avail itself of nuclear technology but it refused to sign the required safeguards agreement with the IAEA until January1992 that would have allowed IAEA inspectors into North Korea's nuclear facilities and would have required it to observe certain safeguards measures. Under the terms of the Safeguards Agreement, North Korea provided an initial declaration of its nuclear facilities and materials, and allowed the IAEA inspectors access to them to verify the completeness and correctness of the initial declaration. Six rounds of inspections began in May 1992 and ended in February 1993.

The initial inspections were conducted by the IAEA Director General, Hans Blix and three IAEA experts. They had been briefed by the CIA and other US experts on three occasions before their departure to North Korea. The highlight of the briefings was the reprocessing facility that North Korea had denied existed. In its initial declaration, Pyongyang said that it had separated only 90 grams of Pu-239 from the spent fuel rods of the 5 MW graphite reactor in 1990. However, when the US Air Force Technology Applications Center at Patrick Air Force Base in Florida analyze the Pu-239 sample that the North Koreans had given Blix, they found that it contained Pu-239 that had been removed from the 5 MW reactor on three different occasions: in 1989, 1990 and 1991, rather than at a single time in 1990 that the North Koreans had claimed.

In 1992 the IAEA received satellite photographs from the United States that showed two buildings at Yongbyon that appeared to be nuclear related, but that Pyongyang had not declared. One was a two story building that had been camouflaged to appear as a one story building. It had been monitored during its construction by US satellites and its lower floor contained large reinforced concrete vaults that are suitable for storing nuclear waste. The top floor was filled with heavy military equipment including tanks. When the IAEA inspectors arrived to inspect the building, they were refused entrance. The North Koreans claimed that the building was a military facility that was exempt from inspections. On November 12, 1992, in a telephone conversation, Hans Blix told Willi Theis, his chief inspector in Yongbyon, that the IAEA had indisputable proof that a trench existed between the "one story building" and the Pu-239 reprocessing facility. Blix instructed Theis to tell the North Koreans that they had to declare both sites as nuclear facilities and allow inspectors to them.

At first Theis tried to get the Koreans to modify their initial declaration, but the Koreans refused and Theis sparred with them for the next three months as the IAEA presented evidence that the purpose of the trench to carry radioactive waste from the reprocessing facility to the "one story building." In late December 1992, Blix requested "visits" to clarify the nature of the two sites. Pyongyang responded saying "a visit by officials could not be turned into an inspection" and that inspections of non-nuclear military facilities "could jeopardize the supreme interests of the DPRK." This was a reference to the NPT clause that allows a party to withdraw from the Treaty to avoid jeopardizing its "supreme national interests."

In preparation for the IAEA Board of Governors meeting in February 1993, Blix asked the United States for permission to show the high-resolution satellite photos of the disputed sites to the Board, but the CIA bureaucracy objected to showing them to the IAEA Board that included members from countries such as Libya, Syria and Algeria and to representatives of North Korea who would be present at the meeting. But CIA Director Robert Gates, overruled his staff because sensitive satellite imagery had been displayed before to the UN Security Council during the Chad crisis in 1980 and during the 1990-1991 Iraq-Kuwaiti crisis. Gates later recalled, "For me, the notion of sharing imagery with an international agency was not as new or as radical as it may have been to the bureaucracy."

Almost a dozen of the high-resolution photographs were displayed at the IAEA board meeting on February 22, 1993. The board was deeply impressed and voted to demand that North Korea allow special inspections "without delay" of the two disputed sites. Blix sent a telegram to North Korea's foreign minister requesting that IAEA inspectors be allowed to inspect the disputed sites on March 16, but the situation grew extremely tense because March 9 was to be the beginning of the US-South Korean joint Team Spirit exercise that would involve 70,000 South Korean troops, and 50,000 US troops that included 19,000 US troops from outside the country, and the deployment of the US aircraft carrier, the USS Independence. The day before, Kim Jong-il, who had succeeded his father a year earlier, ordered the entire nation and its armed forces "to assume a state of readiness for war." He said that the Team Spirit was a "nuclear war test aimed at a surprise, preemptive strike at the northern half of the country." North Korea's senior military officers were told that an attack might be imminent and were ordered to underground fortifications. All military leaves were cancelled, soldier's heads were shaved, and steel helmets and ammunition were issued to them. In the countryside, civilians were ordered to dig trenches and prepare for air attacks, All this was a precursor to North Korea's withdrawal from the NPT, which Pyongyang announced on March 12, citing the "supreme national interest" clause of the Treaty. However, the NPT specifies that a member state must give a ninety days notice of its withdrawal from the treaty before its withdrawal takes effect.

On April 1, the IAEA determined that North Korea was in non-compliance with its Safeguards Agreement and referred the matter to the UN Security Council which unanimously passed Resolution 825 that called upon North Korea to reconsider its decision to withdraw from the NPT, and allow the IAEA inspectors back into the country.

South Korea's new foreign minister, Han Sung Joo, was a former academic with a PhD from the University of California at Berkeley, but with no previous government experience. After learning of Pyongyang's threat to withdraw from the NPT, Han thought that Seoul should negotiate with Pyongyang to cancel its withdrawal. His concerns were: first, that North Korea would produce nuclear weapons; second, that the United States and other countries would react so strongly to cause war to break out on the peninsula; and third, that there would be a popular demand for South Korea acquire its own nuclear weapons that would initiate a nuclear arms race on the peninsula. Han's reaction to the impending crisis was a vaguely formulated "carrot and stick" approach. His carrots included: cancelation of the Team Spirit exercises; security guarantees to North Korea, trade and incentives to cooperate with the international community. His sticks ranged from downgrading or severing diplomatic relations to economic embargos and even military actions.

With these in mind, Han flew to Washington where he found a warm reception at the State Department where its officials had been thinking along similar lines, but his approach was rejected by more conservative and hawkish elements in both Seoul and Washington. The US Joint Chiefs of Staff said, "Under no circumstances should you engage [the North Koreans] in negotiations. You should not reward them. You should punish them."

It soon became apparent that there was no military option, and that negotiations were the only approach even though there was little enthusiasm for them. Because of China's good relations with Pyongyang, Beijing was approached to participate, but Beijing said that the Washington should negotiate directly with Pyongyang, which was eager for direct negotiations with Washington because it would enhance their international standing.

With only a month remaining before the ninety day notification period was up, a member of North Korea's UN delegation in New York telephoned C. Kenneth Quinones, the North Korean office director at the State Department in Washington and asked if the Americans wanted to meet, and if they did, the sooner the better.

With only ten days left before North Korea's withdrawal from the NPT, the negotiations began on June 2 at the United States UN mission in New York. The US negotiator was Robert L. Gallucci, the assistant secretary of state for political-military affairs and

Quinones. The meeting opened with a long monologue by Kang Sok Ju, North Korea's deputy foreign minister. Kang delivered a long monologue that praised the glorious achievements of the Great Leader Kim Jong-il and the glories of North Korea's Juche ideology. But the exchanges that followed produced no results and the American delegation returned to Washington after telling the North Koreans to call them if they wished to continue the discussions.

The call came through and on Monday, June 7, three days before the withdrawal would become effective, Quinones returned to New York and met with three North Korean diplomats in a Fourty-Second Street coffee shop. Quinones and the North Koreans continued their discussions in the coffee shop for the next three days with no apparent progress. During dinner on the eleventh an American member recalled reading an editorial in a North Korean newspaper that contained a formulation suggesting that there were circum-stances in which a solution was possible.

At the meeting the next morning when Gallucci read the newspaper's text to the North Koreans, their eyes lit up and the mood became positive. That afternoon the US diplomats drafted an agreement that included assurances against "the threat and use of force, including nuclear weapons," and against "interference in each other's internal affairs." In lengthy meetings on the tenth and eleventh, Gallucci and Kang hammered out a six paragraph joint statement that became the basis for the Agreed Framework agreement. It included provisions for the United States to provide light water nuclear reactors that could provide two thousand megawatts of electric power.

However, before the agreement was finalized, the negotiations continued in Geneva, Switzerland. The North Koreansobjected to the light water reactors because of their complexity and sophistication, and wanted them replaced with less complex and less proliferation proof gas-graphite modulated reactors that were then in service or under construction in North Korea. The negotiations continued for the net two years while the negotiators haggled over the reactor issue. The North Koreans finally accepted the US position, and signed the Agreed Framework agreement on October 21, 1994. It included the following provisions:

- The United States with supply North Korea with light water nuclear reactors capable of generating approximately 2,000 megawatts of electric power;
- The United States will deliver 500,000 tons of heavy fuel oil annually during th construction of the light water nuclear reactors;
- North Korea will freeze its graphite modulated reactors and complete their dismantling by the time that the construction of the light water reactors is completed;
- North Korea will remain a party to the Nuclear Non-proliferation Treaty and will allow implementation of its Safeguards Agreement and will allow routine inspections of its nuclear facilities;
- The United States and North Korea will move towards the normalization of their political and economic relations;
- Both sides will work towards the peace and security of a nuclear free Korean Peninsula;
- Both sides will work together to strengthen the international nuclear non-proliferation regime.[51]

The Agreed Framework was neither a treaty that would have required ratification by the US Senate, nor a legally binding executive agreement. It was only a non-binding political commitment. The United States regarded the Agreed Framework primarily as a nonproliferation agreement that bound North Korea to the NPT and its commitments in its Safeguards Agreements; whereas North Korea placed greater value on its provisions regarding the normalization of its relations with the United States that it thought would enhance its standing in the international community.

The Demise of the Agreed Framework: In early 2001 the US intelligence community issued an assessment that, based on indirect evidence such as North Korea's purchase of high strength aluminum and high speed electric motors, North Korea was pursuing a uranium enrichment program. James A. Kelly, the assistant secretary of state for East Asian affairs, was planning a trip to Pyongyang in October 2004. However, John Bolton, the conservative under-secretary of state for political-military affairs, was in Seoul in late August and gave bellicose speech that was hostile towards North Korea. North Korea's foreign minister responded, saying, "The DPRK has clarified more than one that if the United States has the will to drop its hostile policies towards the DPRK it would have a dialogue with the United States to clear the United States of its worries about its security."[52]

The Japanese had been informed of the US intelligence assessment and when the Japanese Foreign Minister Junichiro Koizumi met with Kim Jong-il in September, he obliquely raised the enrichment issue, Kim did not respond. It is hard to imagine that Kim Jong-il missed the point was missed.

When Kelly and his delegation arrived in Pyongyang on October 4, his instructions told them not to negotiate, not to hold a dinner for their hosts, and not to engage in normal diplomatic practices that might begin the process to resolving the issue. Pyongyang was to be punished for its "cheating." It is obvious that the instructions had been cleared with Secretary of Defense, Donald Rumsfeld, and Vice President Dick Cheney. The delegation was put on a very short lease.

When Kelly raised the issue of the uranium m enrichment facility during the first meeting in Pyongyang, and despite the likelihood that the North Korean's knew of the American suspicions, the North Koreans appeared to be caught off guard. The head of the Korean delegation, Vice Foreign Minister, Kim Gye Gwan, called for a recess so he could get instructions on how he should respond.

When the meeting resumed, the Vice Foreign Minister said that the charges were false and were an effort by those opposed to improving US-North Korean relations, and that those who were not opposed to North Korea could do business with the PRK, and then he moved on to his prepared presentation.

The North Koreans realized that they had been caught cheating and that there could be no progress until the cheating issue was somehow resolved. When the delegations met in the Ministry of Foreign Affairs conference room, the Americans at the table could not believe their ears when they heard Kang Sok Ju admit that North Korea indeed had an enrichment program. He said that as a sovereign nation the DPRK had a right to possess nuclear weapons for defense and to enrich uranium.

That was the end of the meetings. The Americans went directly to the British embassy to draft their report of the meetings. It was entitled "North Korea Definitely Admits to HEW Program." They sent it to Washington using the British secure communications facilities.

A month later, in November 2004, the United States halted the delivery of the fuel oil and the construction of the light water reactors by the Korean Energy Development Organization (KEDO). Both sides blamed the other for the breakdown of the agreement. On February 10, 2005 Pyongyang announced for a second time that it was withdrawing from the NPT effective the following day.

The Six Party Talks

55ter Pyongyang withdrew from the NPT, President George W. Bush in 2003 became concerned that bilateral relations with North Korea had been a failure in case of the Agreed Framework, and concluded that, only China had enough leverage to convince Kim Jong-il to give up his nuclear weapons. The Bush administration approached Beijing and asked it to organize a multilateral form that would include China, South Korea, Japan and Russia in addition to North Korea and the United States. At first Beijing demurred, saying that Washington should negotiate directly with Pyongyang, but after President Bush telephoned the Chinese President Zang Jemin in March 2003, he told Zang that he was under pressure from hard-liners to use military force and a nuclear Japan could not be ruled out if Pyongyang remained unconstrained. Zang responded by organizing the Six Party Talks that South Korea, Japan and Russia in addition to North Korea and the United States chaired by China.[53]

Representatives of the six nations met for the first time in Beijing for four days from August 27, 2003 until the twenty-ninth. Their only achievement was agreement to meet again. The parties convened again for the second and third rounds for a few days in February and June in 2004. They agreed that the objectives of the talks were the denuclearization of the Korean Peninsula, and the peaceful coexistence of the participating countries and to establish a mechanism for resolving disputes among them.

But the talks hit several roadblocks between the third and fourth rounds when the US Treasury Department placed sanctions on the Banco Delta Asia bank in Macao that was laundering millions of dollars for North Korea. The Macao government froze about fifty accounts held by North Korean entities. Pyongyang then launched a satellite using its Taepodong-2 missile and restarted its 5 MW plutonium producing rector at Pyongyang that it had suspended operating the reactor's operation during the talks.

The fourth round took place between July 26 and September 16, 2005 with a five week break so the participants could attend the meeting of the Association of the South East Asian Nations (ASEAN). During this round, the parties issued a Joint Statement that they had reached agreement on the following objectives for the Six Party Talks:

- a commitment for the verifiable denuclearization of the Korean Peninsula;
- North Korea would abandon its nuclear weapons program and to rejoin the NPT as soon as possible;
- the five other parties would recognize North Korea's right to pursue the peaceful use of nuclear energy, but the parties could not agree on what the phrase, "the peaceful use of nuclear energy" included;
- the United States would affirm that it had no intention to attack or invade North Korea, and would provide security guarantees to that effect;
- the United States and Japan would normalize their relations with North Korea and to respect each other's sovereignty;
- the other five parties will undertake to promote economic cooperation with North Korea in energy, trade and investment.
- South Korea reaffirmed its proposal to supply North Korea with two million kilowatts of electricity if North Korea abandons its nuclear arms program;
- to negotiate a peace treaty that would end the Korean War.

The fifth round of the Six Party Talks took place between November 2005 and February 2007, but it was broken into three phases. During the first phase from November 9 and November 11, 2005, the parties issued a joint statement that simply reaffirmed the commitments made during the fourth round. On July 4, Pyongyang announced that it would not return to the talks unless the United States would release the funds frozen in Banco Delta Asia bank.

Then in early October there were indications that Pyongyang was preparing for an underground nuclear test, which took place during the morning of October 9 at Mount Mantap 12 km north of the town of Punggye-ri. The Chinese President Hu Jintao called President Bush and complained that the Chinese had given him only an hour alert of the test.,[54]

The international community was stunned by the test and responded in the UN Security Council by unanimously passing Resolution 1718 that condemned the test and imposed sanctions on North Korea that ranged from economic and trade sanctions to sanctions on military related items, including weapons of mass destruction and technology transfers. China, however, refused to allow livelihood sanctions on food and fuel oil. for fear that depriving North Korea of these items might cause the Pyongyang regime to collapse and bring South Korea with 28,500 US troops to its border and tens of thousands of refugees clambering to get into China. The resolution also gave member nations the right to inspect North Korean vessels and aircraft, although China feared that these sanctions could lead to a military confrontation which China sought to avoid.

After intense pressure on Pyongyang by China, the talks resumed on December 28, 2006 for four days during which the parties reaffirmed their commitments to the agreed statement of the first phase. The United States held bilateral discussions with the other parties to freeze North Korea's financial assets in their countries. A meeting to coordinate the freeze of North Korea's financial assets took place in New York on January 22 and 23, 2007. The third phase of the fifth round resumed on February 8, 2007 for five days during which North Korea promised to shut down its five MW graphite modulated reactor and its reprocessing facility, and allow IAEA inspectors into Yongbyon to conduct monitoring and verification inspections. In return, the other parties agreed to provide North Korea with 500,000 tons of fuel oil annually and the release of the $ 25 million frozen Banko Delta Asia funds. However, no bank wanted to touch the money for fear of being accused of money laundering, until a small Russian bank was found that was willing to transfer the money back to North Korea.[55] The parties also agreed to establish five working groups on: the denuclearization of the Korea Peninsula; the normalization of relations between North Korea and the United States and Japan; cooperation on economic and energy issues; and, on establishing of a Northeast Asia peace and security mechanism.

Pyongyang began to dismantle the Yongbyon 5 MW reactor removing thousands of fuel rods under US supervision, and made more concessions by providing a detailed description of its nuclear programs. The Bush administration responded by easing some of the sanctions and removing North Korea from the US list of state sponsors of terrorism. But the Six Party Talks ended at the end of 2008 when Pyongyang refused to agree to the verification protocol for its nuclear facilities.

When the sixth round of the Six Party Talks opened on March 19, 2007, Christopher Hill, the US negotiator, announced that the $ 25 million of frozen funds at Banco Delta Asia were being released because of the positive steps that Pyongyang had taken in dismantling its nuclear facilities and readmitting the IAEA inspectors. But the Bank of China refused to accept the funds from Banco Delta Asia because the bank was on the US List of institutions that supported terrorism. North Korea's representative refused to take part in the negotiations until North Korea had received the funds, and the talks adjourned on March 22. On June 11, Russia agreed to advance the funds to North Korea, and the talks resumed on July 18, but no substantive progress was made and the second phase which lasted only four days was the last meeting of the Six Party Talks

On April 5, 2009, North Korea attempted to launch a satellite despite international pressure not to do so. The United States thought that the launch was a test of an ICBM under the guise of a satellite launch, but the attempt was a failure. President Barack Obama responded, saying "violations must be punished." The UN Security Council condemned North Korea for the launch and stated its intention to apply new sanctions on North Korea. Pyongyang responded by saying that it would "never again take part in such talks and will not be bound by any agreement reached in the talks." North Korea expelled the IAEA inspectors and declared that it was restarting its nuclear weapons program, and that ended the Six Party Talks.

The Leap Day Agreement

Early in 2009 the new Obama administration signaled that it was willing to engage Pyongyang in the resumption of the Six Party Talks, but North Korea responded in May 2009 with its second nuclear weapons test. Washington began to push for tougher sanctions in the UN Security Council. to which Pyongyang responded by continuing its belligerency, sinking a South Korean naval vessel, shelling the South Korean island of Yeonpyeong.

After Kim Song-il died on December 11, 2011 and his thirty-three year son Kim Jong-un assumed power, the Obama administration thought there might be a change in North Korea's attitudes since Kim Jong-un had been educated in Switzerland and he might have acquired a more western liberal outlook. So in July and October 2011 Washington and Pyongyang discussed resuming the Six Party Talks but the new Kim Jong-un regime said that it would only resume the talks with no preconditions which was unacceptable to Washington and Seoul that wanted

Pyongyang to demonstrate its commitment to abandoning its nuclear weapons program as a precondition for resuming talks.

At that time, North Korea was suffering a serious food shortage. In March 2011, the World Food Organization said that more than six million North Koreans urgently needed food aid and that a third of its children under five years of age were seriously malnourished.

The Obama administration thought it might be a propitious time to approach Pyongyang about a trade of its nuclear weapons and missile programs for food aid. In late February 2012 US and North Korean negotiators met in the North Korean embassy in Beijing and quickly reach an agreement under which North Korea "agreed to implement a moratorium on long missile launches, nuclear tests and [other] nuclear activities at Yongbyon, including its uranium enrichment activities."[56] In exchange, the United States agreed to supply North Korea with 240,000 tons of "nutritional assistance with the prospect of additional assistance based on continued need," provided that North Korea complied with its commitments. North Korea had asked for much more food than the United States was willing to supply and wanted it in the form of grain that could be used to feed its million-man army, rather than in the form of "nutritional aid" such as com-soy gruel which would have been far less attractive for diversion to military mess halls and the black market.[57]

The Leap Day Agreement acquired its name because it was signed on February 29, 2012, but the agreement lasted less than two months when Pyongyang announced that it intended to launch a satellite with the banned Taepodong-2 ICBM and that was the end of the Leap Day Agreement.

Chapter V

Punishing North Korea

After each of North Korea's six nuclear tests and its December 2012 satellite launch, the UN Security Council unanimously passed a series of eight resolutions that imposed an increasingly sever regime of sanctions on North Korea. These sanctions are included: in Security Council Resolutions 1718 passed on October 14, 2006 after North Koreas first nuclear test, Resolution 1874 pasted on June 12, 2009 after North Korea's second nuclear test; Resolution 2087 passed on January 22, 2013 after the North Korean satellite launch; Resolution 2321 passed on November 30, 2016 after North Korea's fifth nuclear test and Resolution 2371 passed on August 5, 2017 after North Korea's two long range missile on July 3 and 28, 917, and Resolution 2375 after North Korea's sixth and most powerful nuclear test on September 3, 2017.

Prior to passing Resolution 1718 in 2006, the Security Council passed several resolutions that condemned North Korea's nuclear weapons and missile activities. In response to North Korea's announcement of its intent to withdraw from the NPT in 1993, the Security Council passed Resolution 825 that urged North Korea to remain a party to the NPT, and to honor its obligations under the Treaty. Resolution 1698 was passed in 2006 in response to its ballistic missile launched in July. It called upon North Korea to refrain from such launches.

These resolutions contain three kinds of sanctions: those imposed directly on North Korea, those that call upon the UN member states to refrain from certain activities with North Korea and those that call upon member states to undertake punitive actions on North Korea.

Sanctions imposed directly on North Korea demand that North Korea:

- cease its nuclear weapons and ballistic missile tests;
- rejoin the Nuclear Nonproliferation Treaty (NPT) and reinstate its safeguards agreement with the International Atomic Energy Agency (IAEA);
- abandon all its weapons of its mass destruction programs including its chemical and biological weapons programs in a complete, verifiable and irreversible manner;
- return to the Six Party Talks;
- cease its export of all military items including missiles, missile systems, battle tanks, armored combat vehicles, large caliber artillery pieces, combat aircraft, attack helicopters, warships and all materials, goods, equipment and technology associated with the above items;
- crease the sale, supply or transfer of coal, iron ore, iron, copper, nickel, silver, lead, zinc, to any state directly or indirectly, by its nationals or using its vessels or aircraft.

North Korea has not complied with any of these demands and has developed ingenious methods to evade them that are described below. Furthermore, UN Security Council Resolution 2321 contains a "livelihood exception," loophole which was inserted by China, that allows North Korea to export iron and iron ore if the ban on its export were to cause the North Korean exporter a "livelihood hardship" so long as the revenue from these exports is not used to support of North Korea's nuclear weapons and missile programs. The livelihood exception is self-certified by the exporting individual or company and amounts to a loophole in the sanctions regime and could be tightened or removed.

Resolution 1718 established a Sanctions Committee composed of the fifteen members of the Security Council in October 2006 to function as a monitoring body to review and adjust the imposed sanctions and violations of them. The monitoring body provides a report on the implementation of the sanctions every ninety days. Resolution 1874 established a seven member Panel of Experts to assist the Sanctions Committee in monitoring and enforcing the sanctions. Resolution 2087 directs the Sanctions Committee to issue an Implementation Assistance Notice if a vessel refuses to allow an inspection authorized by its flag state.

The sanction resolutions also call upon the UN member states to take specific actions that prevent or make it difficult for North Korea to pursue its nuclear weapons, ballistic missile and other weapons of mass destruction (WMD) programs including its chemical and biological weapons programs. Member states are prohibited from the "direct or indirect supply, sale or transfer" to North Korea of:

- heavy weaponry such as tanks, armored vehicles, large caliber artillery, combat aircraft, attack helicopters, warships and missile systems;
- small arms and light weapons;
- servicing and repairing any weaponry sold to a third country;
- spare parts for the above weaponry;
- materials and technology that could contribute to North Korea's WMD programs and ballistic missile related activities;
- luxury goods;

- specialized teaching or training of North Korean nationals in disciplines that could contribute to North Korea's proliferation of nuclear or missile technology;
- coal in amounts that exceed an annual cap.

Member states are required to:

- freeze the funds or financial assets of entities designated by the Security Council that provide support for North Korea's nuclear, missile and other WMD programs;
- block cash transfers to and from North Korea;
- restrict North Korea's access to the international banking system;
- limit the number of bank accounts held by North Korean missions and diplomats;
- suspend scientific and technical cooperation with North Korea, except for medial purposes;
- inspect all cargo destined to or originating from North Korea;
- freeze assets on all North Korean government and Worker's Party entities associated with prohibited activities;
- refrain from hosting North Korean financial institutions that may be supporting proliferation activities in North Korea;
- refrain from opening new financial institutions or bank accounts in North Korea;
- terminate existing joint ventures with North Korean entities;
- refrain from chartering or leasing vessels to Noprth Korea, or providing crew services to North Korean entities;
- refrain from selling or supplying aviation fuel to North Korea;
- reduce the number of staff at North Korean diplomatic missions and consular posts

Member states are authorized to

- inspect North Korean cargo on land, sea and air, if the state has reason to believe that the cargo contains prohibited items and seize any prohibited materials or technologies;
- prohibit bunkering services for North Korean ships if the state has reason to believe the ship is carrying illicit materials;
- refuse new loans or credit to North Korea except for humanitarian or development purposes;
- monitor individuals and entities associated with the North Korean regime;
- inspect and detain any suspect cargo or shipments to or from North Korea that transit through its territory if the suspect cargo contains bulk cash or material that could be used in a nuclear program

Following North Korea's sixth nuclear weapons test on September 3, 2017, the UN Security Council unanimously passed Resolution 2375 on September 11. The United States originally proposed that the resolution prohibit the provision of fuel oil, natural gas and refined petroleum products to North Korea, but both China and Russia objected, so a compromise was reached with limits North Korea's imports of refined and crude oil to 8.5 million barrels annually which reduced North Korea's supply of these commodities by thirty percent. The resolution also prohibits North Korea from exporting textiles which will reduce North Korea's income by $720 million annually, which amounts to more than a quarter of North Korea's exports. A separate agreement prohibits member states from renewing guest worker contracts which will deprive North Korea of another $ 500 million annually. Another provision of UNSCR 2375 allows member states to demand the inspection of ships suspected of carrying North Korean goods. The United States originally proposed that such ships could be challenged with military force, but that was dropped to avoid a veto by China or Russia.[58]

China has supported all these sanctions except it did not allow sanctions that would prevent North Korea from importing food and fuel oil because China fears that shortages of these items could cause the collapse of the Pyongyang regime that would bring South Korea to its border with the 28,500 US troops stationed in South Korea. China regards North Korea a buffer between it and South Korea.[59]

In addition to these sanctions, South Korea, Japan, the European Union and the United States have imposed their own sanctions on North Korea. The US sanctions: require the President to sanction entities that have contributed to North Korea's weapons of mass destruction programs, arms trade, human rights violations and other illegal activities; requires the Treasury Department to determine whether North Korea should be listed as a "primary money laundering concern" which would trigger tough new sanctions; prohibit North Korean banks from processing transactions through the US banking system; and imposed new sanctions on North Korea for its human rights abuses. However, the Bush administration removed North Korea from its list of state sponsors of terrorism in February 2007 during the sixth round of the Six Party Talks.

South Korea's sanctions ban North Korean ships from South Korean territorial waters; suspends trade with North Korea except at the Kaesong Industrial Park; and bans most cultural exchanges. Japan's sanctions include: a ban on remittances to North Korea except for humanitarian purposes, but these cannot exceed 100,000 yen ($ 990) in value; freezes the assets of suspect individuals and organizations in Japan; bans North Korean ships and other ships that have visited North Korea from Japanese ports; bans nuclear and missile technicians that been to North Korea from entering Japan.

The European Union sanctions include: a ban on the export of aviation and rocket fuel to North Korea; an embargo on all arms and related materials; a ban on the trade of gold, precious metals and diamonds with the North Korean government; a ban on the import of minerals, except for coal and iron ore, from North Korea; and a prohibition on certain North Korean individuals from entering the European Union.

North Korea Sanction Evasion Activities

Despite sanctions to punish and isolate North Korea, Pyongyang has been able to evade many of these sanctions through increasingly sophisticated and diversified techniques. Many developing and under developed countries in Africa, South Asia and South America either do not observe the sanctions on North Korea or profess to not be aware of them and continued to trade with North Korea which became more profitable. Thus, North Korea has become a major supplier of small arms, ammunition, grenades, grenade launchers, military communications equipment and chemical weapons to war torn underdeveloped and developing countries around the world. China's Foreign Minister Wang YI recently described North Korea's actions as "swords drawn and bows bent."

North Korea operates through a network of front companies; and it uses foreigners to conceal Pyongyang's prohibited activities. It has been able to buy and sell most of the illicit items in the international black markets, by establishing front companies in countries such as Singapore, Malaysia and China and by embedding its agents and intermediaries in foreign trading companies in other countries. Pyongyang has been able to trade in illicit goods with countries such as Pakistan, Iran, Syria and Libya. It has been able to use the international financial system, airlines and container shipping routs. Pyongyang has developed relationships with trusted foreign nationals. It also trades through some African countries that do not enforce the UN sanctions or are unaware of them.[60]

One example of Pyongyang's flagrant evasion of the prohibition of luxury goods is when Kin Jong-un and his entourage arrived at his April 15, 2017 military parade in a fleet of Mercedes Benz Maybachs luxury sedans, an $ 80,000 automobile.[61]

Pan Systems Pyongyang is an international trading company at the center of Pyongyang's evasion activities. It had maintained two front companies in Malaysia: International Golden Services Sdn Bhd and International Global Systems Sdn Bhd. Until recently North Korean nationals have had visa free access to Malaysia, but after the assassination of Kim Song-un's half brother in Kuala Lumpur, Malaysian authorities required North Korean nationals to obtain visas to enter the country. Early in March 2017, the Malaysian police closed the two firms "to insure that Malaysia is not used for activities detrimental to its national security." Glocom is another front company that markets North Korean made radio equipment for military and paramilitary units abroad.[62]

Nearly 93,000 North Koreans are employed abroad as laborers and are forced to send a large portion of their wages back to Pyongyang that amounts to more than $ 2.3 billion annually59 that can be used to purchase illicit items on the international black markets. Clothing factories in Dandong, China at the mouth of the Yalu River employ more than 10,000 North Korean workers who work twelve to fourteen hours a day and are paid no more than $ 260 a month. Approximately three times that amount, or $ 93 million annually, goes to Pyongyang. Another 83,000 North Koreans are employed in fourty countries. North Korea earns an additional $ 70 million annually by selling rights to foreign fishermen to fish in its waters.[63]

Pyongyang has established more than twenty front companies and agents in China that between 2013 and 2016 dealt with 5,233 Chinese companies to buy necessary components and raw materials and to sell completed items through these Chinese firms. In 2016 China accounted for about 85 percent of North Korea's foreign trade, and ten firms accounted for just shy of 30 percent of imports from North Korea. One firm, the Dandong Hongxiang Industrial Development Company Ltd. described itself as, "an enterprise that conducts Sino-North Korean imports and exports [that] accounts for more than twenty percent of market share."[64]

To finance these operations Pan Systems Pyongyang maintains bank accounts in China, Malaysia, Singapore, Indonesia and in the Middle East. By conducting financial transactions through these entities and under such names as Pan Systems Singapore, Pyongyang has been able to maintain access to the international financial system to finance its prohibited activities. Many of these transactions go through US correspondent banks in New York.[65]

Although China has vowed to fully enforce the sanctions against North Korea, Beijing has had trouble doing so. It has been unable to enforce its anticorruption laws against domestic graft, bribery and corruption, let alone monitoring and punishing North Koran miscreants. North Korea has been able to infiltrate Chinese banks and trading firms with agents who can bribe officials in these institutions to launder money and facilitate trades to pass through these trading firms. Chin's economy is heavily oriented towards exports and enforcing these laws against tens of thousands of companies engaged in export-import trading has proved extremely difficult for the Chinese authorities.

Graft, bribery and corruption have a long tradition and has been an integral part of China culture. dating back to at least Sung Dynasty (960 – 1279 CE) when wealthy merchants could buy literary degrees that would make them eligible to become officials such as provincial governors in the imperial government. Scholars who passed the imperial examinations may have studied the

Chinese classics from the age of six, some-times to the age of thirty.65 During the later years of the Qing Dynasty (1644 -1911 CE), the salary of a governor of a province as large as France or Spain might be paid as little as $ 1,000 a year (in terms of today's standard) by the provincial treasury. This would be increased by an imperial supplement of $ 125,000 a year. And to this would be added funds obtained by the "squeeze" and nepotism system. In the "squeeze" system junior officials give their superiors "gifts" increasing the income of the senior many times his official income.66

Today such corruption and graft continues to be pervasive throughout China. President Xi Jinping has initiated an anti-corruption campaign in which some 270,000 cadres were prosecuted and imprisoned between 2012 and 2016. Most have been low and mid-level party members and functionaries. But it has also included members of the Politburo. Although Xi's anticorruption campaign is widely supported, it has run into resistance from many parts of Chinese society including Xi's two immediate predecessors, Jiang Zemin and Hu Jintao.67

As Beijing has become more and more aggravated with Pyongyang's sanction evasion activities, Russian smugglers have moved in to replace reductions in Chinese fuel exports to North Korea. A marked increase in tanker traffic between Russia's east coast port of Vladivostok and the North Korean port of Rajin has been observed. The tankers carry mostly diesel and other fuels. Russians have established a front company, Velmus, in Singapore that is registered as a as a real estate management company, , but its real function appears to be "facilitation the laundering of funds for North Korea financial facilitators and sanctioned entities," according to the US Treasury Department. These activities appear to be with the approval of the Russian government. In a joint news conference with South Korea's President Moon Jae-in, Russia's President Vladimir Putin pointedly refused to support the new sanctions on fuel to North Korea. He said, "We should not act out of emotion and push North Korea to a dead end."[68]

Secondary Sanctions: One way of increasing the effectiveness of sanctions on Pyongyang would be by using secondary sanctions which are sanctions imposed on individuals and firms—primarily banks and other financial institutions—that do business with a sanctioned country. This approach was effective with Iran. Despite the primary sanctions on Iran, hundreds of foreign banks were doing business with Iranian banks. Kunlun Bank, a Chinese based bank, was providing millions of dollars worth of financial services to a half dozen sanctioned Iranian banks. Despite repeated warnings to Beijing, China's Kunlun Bank refused to curtail its activities, so in 2012, the US Treasury Department cut off Kunlun Bank's access to US banks, and it did the same with Elaf Islamic Bank in Iraq. Beijing responded to the Kunlun activity by issuing a routine, tepid complaint, but it told Kunlun to stop dealing with the Iranian banks. A few large banks including Barclays, Credit Suisse, ING and Lloyds then stopped their dealings with Iranian banks for fear that Washington would restrict them as it had done for the Kunlun and Elaf banks.[69]

With regards to North Korea, the United States had applied secondary sanctions to Banko Delta Asia in Macao that was laundering money for Pyongyang, but North Korea primarily uses smaller Chinese banks for its foreign financial transactions, If the US Treasury Department applied secondary sanctions to one or several of these banks, Beijing might respond as it did in the case of Iran, but it might not because China's interests in North Korea are much different than they were with respect to Iran. If the United States were to use this approach with respect to North Korea, it would best coordinate these actions with Beijing first.[70]

Chapter VI

Kim Il-sung's Juche Ideology:

In response to the difficult relations that developed between Pyongyang and Beijing, Tokyo, Moscow and Washington, in the mid-1960s Kim Il-sung adopted the political ideology of Juche which became the official state ideology of North Korea. Juche is usually translated as self-reliance. Kim Il-sung explained juche thusly:

Establishing juche means, in a nutshell, being the master of revolution and reconstruction in one's own country. This means holding fast to an independent position, rejecting dependence on others, using one's own brains, believing in one's own strength, displaying the revolutionary spirit of self-reliance, and thus solving one's own problems for one's own self on one's own responsibility under all circum-stances.[71]

Pyongyang claims that juche is Kim Il-sung's application of Marxist-Leninist principles to the contemporary realities of North Korea. However, the term and its concept of juche can be traced back to the Korean scholars of the early twentieth century.[72] Juche is based on the Korean principle that "man is the master over all things who creates his own destiny," and it views the Korean people as the chosen ones. But according to Kim Il-sung, the chosen people must be guided by the Great Leader, who, in an analogy to the human body, is the brain that makes decisions and commands action, and the People's Workers Party is the nervous system that transmits the Great Leaders commands to the workers who are the mussels and bones of the system. Kim Il-sung and his son Kim Jong-il have indoctrinated the North Korean people with the juche ideology and has mobilize them into a fiercely nationalistic force able to withstand famines and economic stagnation. The Kims have also used juche to justify North Korea's ideological independence from both China and Russia despite the fact that China supplies 90 percent of North Korea's fuel oil and 45 percent of its food. They view their nuclear weapons and missiles as the guarantor of North Korea's political, economic and military independence which Kim Il-sung elaborated in his December 16, 1967 address,

> Let us Defend the Revolutionary Spirit of Independence, Self-Reliance and Self-Defense More Thoroughly in All Fields of State Activity, . . . [T]he Government of the Republic will implement with all consistency the line of independence, self-sustenance , and self-defense to consolidate the political independence of the country, build up more solidly of an independent national economy capable of insuring the complete unification, independence and prosperity of our nation and increasing the country's defense capabilities, so as to safeguard the security of the fatherland reliability by our own force, by splendidly embodying our Party's idea of juche in all fields.[73]

Because of North Korea's supposed independence in its international relations as embodied in the juche ideology, Pyongyang cannot rely on the assistance of others despite its dependence on China for its oil and food needs. According to the juche ideology, to yield to foreign pressures or to accept outside aid would make it impossible for North Korea to maintain its independence. Yet practical necessity forces North Korea to violate its own political ideology.

Juche also means that North Korea's citizens must fortify themselves against famine and even starvation. But Kim Il--sung recognized that his country is not able to survive without outside help, so he encouraged economic and technical cooperation with friendly socialist countries such as China and the Soviet Union to help his country's economic development and to assure its ideological unity.[74]

For Juche, independence and self reliance also means the independence of the sovereign state which implies a strong national defense. Kim Il-sung once said, "We do not want war, nor are we afraid of it. Nor do we beg for peace from imperialists." He was adamant in countering any perceived "imperialist moves of aggression and war" against his country which required a strong army and a self-reliant defense that would involve the mobilization of the entire country, and the inoculation of the juche principles into the armed forces. Thus, his people had to be ideologically and materially prepared to cope with war relying only on their own resources.[75]

From a very young age, North Korean children are indoctrinated with the juche ideology and are propagandized with it during the rest of their lives. Every household has a radio tuned to a single station that broadcasts government propaganda throughout the day. Although these radios cannot be turned off, their volume can be adjusted and reduced. All journalists and broadcasters are required to follow Kim Jong-il's book, Guidance for Journalists that instructs them to "carry articles in which they unfailingly hold the president in high esteem, adore him and praise him as the great revolutionary leader. Except for a few thousand elites, North Koreans have no access to the internet outside of their country. Instead there is a closed domestic system, the Kwangmyong, that is available in schools and libraries, but it is heavily censored. However foreign material that is deemed safe enough for domestic consumption such as scientific and health related materials may be added to the domestic system.[76]

To inculcate all North Koreans with the juche ideology, Kim Jong-il, in 1974, prorogated the ten principles for the Establishment of the One-Ideology System which requires all North Koreans to acknow-ledge the absolute authority of the Great Leader and to pledge total obedience to the state. Kim Jong-il required that all North Koreans memorize these principles and follow them in their daily lives. From the first grade on they are required to attend weekly "self criticism" sessions and engage in peer surveillance. In these meetings, held in offices, classrooms and factories, the participants recite the ten principles and are called upon to criticize both themselves and one another for failing to live in perfect compliance with the ten principles of juche.[77]

Chapter VII

Relations

Inter-Korean Relations

Relations between the two Koreas have alternated between extreme hostility and suspicious cooperation. During the late 1960s a series of low level armed clashes, known as the Korean DMZ Conflict, occurred across the Demilitarized Zone. On January 28, 1968, North Korean commandos attacked the Blue House in Seoul, the official residence and executive offices of South Korea's president, and on December 11, 1969 North Korean agents hijacked a South Korea airliner and flew it to North Korea. Two months later 39 of its passengers were released, but the four crew members and seven other passengers were kept by Pyongyang.

Then relations seemed to improve during the 1970s when South Korea's President Park Chung-hee secretly contacted Kim Il-sung, and in August 1971 talks between North and South Korean Red Crosses took place. But the participants also included intelligence agents and other government officials from both sides. Then in May 1972 the director of South Korea's CIA met secretly with Kim Il-sung in Pyongyang, who apologized for the Blue House attack saying that he had not approved it. North Korea's deputy primer made a return visit to Seoul, and on July 4, 1972 a joint statement was issued that announced the Three Principle of Reunification. But Pyongyang suspended the reunification talks after the kidnapping of Kim Dae-jung, South Korea's opposition leader, by South Korea's CIA in Tokyo in August 1973. The talks resumed later in 1973 but they were abandoned in 1975.

In 1983 Pyongyang proposed three way talks with Seoul and Washington, but they failed to materialize because of an assassination attempt on South Korea's president in Rangoon, Burma. Then in September 1984 North Korea's Red Cross sent emergency supplies to South Korea after severe floods ravished the country. After Seoul was chosen as the site of the 1988 Summer Olympics, Pyongyang tried to convince its communist allies to boycott the games. When that failed, Pyongyang arranged for the hijacking and bombing of Korean Air flight 858 on November 29, 1987. But despite this tragic event which cost 104 passengers and 11 crew members their lives, the newly elected South Korean President Roh Tae-woo launched his Nordpolitik initiative which proposed the formation of a "Korean Community," which paralled Pyongyang's previous proposal for a Korean Confederation. Talks at the ministerial level were held in Seoul between September 4 and 7, 1990, at the same time that Pyongyang was protesting Moscow's normalization of relations with Seoul. Nevertheless, the talks in Seoul led to the 1991 Agreement on Reconciliation, Non-Aggression, Exchanges and Cooperation, and to the joint declaration on the Denuclearization of the Korean Peninsula after the withdrawal of the US tactical nuclear weapons from South Korea in 1991. It was during this period that both countries were admitted as members to the United Nations.

On March 23, 1991, the unified Korean table tennis team displayed the Korean Unification Flag at the World Table Tennis Competition in Japan, and in May 1991, a unified Korean soccer team competed in the World Youth Soccer Competition in Portugal.

But these goodwill initiatives began to unravel in 1994 over disagreements over the North's nuclear weapons program and the collapse of the Framework Agreement between Pyongyang and Washington and Pyongyang's withdrawal from the NPT in 2003. About this time, North Korea began to experience a famine crisis that caused more than ten thousand of its citizens to flee to the South.

In 1998 South Korean President Kim Dae-ung announced his Sunshine Policy towards North Korea that resulted in the first Inter-Korean summit between Presidents Kim Dae-ung and Kim Il-sung in June 2000 in Pyongyang, and for which Kim Dae-ung was awarded the 2000 Nobel Peace Prize. The summit resulted in the reunions of families that had been separated for over fifty years since the division of Korea in 1945. In September 2000, the North Korean and South Korean Olympic teams marched together during the Sydney Olympic Games. Trade between the North and South increased to the point at which South Korea became the North's largest trading partner.

The two sides formed a joint venture to develop the Mount Kungang tourist region in North Korea, and in 2003 they undertook the joint venture to develop the Kaesong Industrial Park located six miles north of the demilitarized zone. It was established as a joint venture between South Korea's Hyundai Company and the North Korean government that allowed South Korean businessmen to invest in the North and to hire North Korean workers at low wages. In April 2013, 123 South Korean companies employed 53,000 North Korean workers. Their wages totaled US $ 93 million annually in hard currency that went directly to the North Korean government that then paid the workers in local North Korean currency.

After North Korea launched its satellite in January 2013, conducted its third nuclear test the following month and then threatened "the final destruction of South Korea" at a UN disarmament conference, Pyongyang refused to let southerners into the Park and in April 2013, Pyongyang removed all its workers from the Park. Then on February 10, 2016 South Korea's Minister of Unification announced that the park would be temporally closed in protest to the January 2016 nuclear test. The next day Pyongyang expelled all Southern personnel from the park and confiscated all the South's assets at the Park.

In November 2009, North and South Korean naval vessels exchanged fire in the Yellow Sea. On March 26, 2010, the North Korean navy torpedoed the South Korean warship, Cheonan, killing forty-six of its sailors, and then on November 23, 2010 North Korea shelled the South Korean island of Yeonpyeong-do resulting in two military and two civilian deaths. Because of these incidents, Seoul terminated all trade with North Korea.

In March 2014 South Korea recovered a crashed North Korean drone aircraft. Its cameras contained pictures of the Blue House and military installations just south of the DMZ. In August 2015, a land mine exploded in the DMZ wounding two South Korean soldiers. Seoul accused the North of planting the land mine which Pyongyang denied. Then on August 20, 2015, North Korean fired an artillery shell on the South Korean city of Yeoncheon. South Korea fired several rounds in response. A meeting was convened at Panmunjom on August 22 to resolve the tensions, but the next day while the talks were in progress, North Korea deployed seventy percent of its submarines thus increasing tensions. The Panmunjom talks continued until August 25 when an agreement was reached and military tensions were finally relaxed.

North and South Koreas' Positions on Reunification: The leaders of both Koreas have expressed their desires for a reunified Korea. On July 4, 1972 Kim Il-sung and the South Korean leader Park Chung-hee issued a joint statement agreeing that the two Koreas should seek reunification based on the Three Principles of

Reunification: "first, reunification must be solved independently without interference from or reliance on foreign powers; second, reunification must be realized in a peaceful way without armed forces against each other; and third, unification transcends the differences in ideology and institutions to promote the unification of Korea as one ethnic group." The talks continued for about a year during which Seoul and Pyongyang established a hot line, but the talks were suspended by Pyongyang in 1973 after the opposition leader in South Korea was kidnapped. On the June 15, 2000 Seoul and Pyongyang issued a Joint Declaration in which they agreed to work together for the peaceful reunification in the future. However, they have vastly different ideas about how this should be. achieved and what the outcome should be.

Ever since the division of Korea, every South Korean government has maintained that "unification and the birth of a unitary government shall be realized through general elections based on liberal democracy and the market economy." On January 6, 2014, South Korea's President Park Geun-hye held a press conference in which she said, "building a foundation for an era of unification as one of two state affairs for 2014." She said that "Preparations must be made to break away from the inter-Korean confrontation, threats of war, nuclear threats, to open an era of unification and policies will be promoted to resolve North Korea's nuclear issue, strengthen humanitarian aid for North Korean citizens, and expand civic exchanges."[78]

Reunification has been a major obsession of North Korea's rulers since the division of Korea in 1945, and they have maintained two unyielding principles regarding unification: first, the division of Korea was the result of "knifing imperialists;" and second, the issue of unification is the problem of realizing the independence of the nation as a single country.[79] But given the vast differences between the two systems, it is almost impossible that either would ever agree to a unification under the other's terms.

Thus the only way that unification could be achieved is through an armed conflict.

In his New Years address on January 1, 2014 Kim Jong-un said, "new progress must be made on the unification of the motherland . . . in accordance with the last wishes of Kim Song-il and Kim Il-sung." But he also said that South Korea and the United States are "staging frantic exercises to practice for a nuclear war attack on North Korea and a dangerous environment is brewing in which even a minor military conflict can turn into an all-out war." In Pyongyang's view, unification can only be achieved by South Korea denouncing the United States, expelling the anti-unification forces and it must be grounded on "By-Our-Nation-Itself ideal." The "nation" that Pyongyang envisions is an exclusive isolated nation imbedded with a class consciousness.[80]

Seoul's Responses to North Korea's Threats: In an opinion poll by the South Korean Yonhap News Agency taken shortly after North Korea's fourth nuclear test in January 2016, 52.5 percent of the respondents expressed doubts about the reliability of the US extended nuclear deterrence to retaliate with its nuclear weapons if Pyongyang were to attack South Korea with its nuclear weapons, and that South Korea should develop its own independent nuclear deterrence. Within South Korea's Saenuri ruling party there are rising pro-nuclear sentiments. Wen Yoo-chui, the party's parliamentary leader, has said that South Korea should not be bound by the Nuclear Nonproliferation Treaty. He and his followers argue: first, that an independent nuclear weapons capability would be a more credible deterrent than depending on the US nuclear umbrella and pointed to the French example; second, it would correct the imbalance between South and North Korea; and third, it would put pressure on China and the United States, to act more forcefully to achieve denuclearization of North Korea.[81] Given the widespread fear that

China and the United States are not sufficiently committed to dealing with the challenge from the North, South Koreans fear that they will be left alone to cope with the North Korean threat. As one South Korean academic put it, "If we give up securing our own nuclear deterrent for fear of international opposition and depend unilaterally on the United States, we will become no more than a chess piece to be manipulated by the big powers." But few of the nuclear advocates go so far as to actively advocate that South Korea initiate a nuclear weapons program then, but are asking that the government consider the nuclear option. They advocate the development of a "non-military," civil enrichment and reprocessing capability as a hedge for a future nuclear weapons program.[82]

But opposition to going nuclear is also strong among government officials, the military and the public. When asked if South Korea would go nuclear, a senior military official responded, "For certain, that will not happen." The head of the editorial board of a leading South Korean newspaper said that a nuclear weapons program would "throw South Korea back into the Stone Age" by undermining its reputation as a champion of nonproliferation making it impossible to press North Korea to denuclearize, precipitating the departure of US forces, and damaging the economy that is heavily dependent on foreign trade. One official argued that "going nuclear was incompatible with existing Republic of Korea-United States alliance arrangements," and another argued that it was also incompatible with the goal of unifying the peninsula.[83]

The Chinese-North Korean Relations

The relationship between North Korea and China is a complex and changing one. On one hand, China supports North Korea because it forms a buffer between it and the democratic South Korea where some 28,500 US troops are stationed, and where the United States has deployed the THAAD missile defense system that carry fourty-eight interceptor missiles. But China also fears that a collapse of North Korea would cause an overwhelming influx of refugees trying to enter China and would bring South Korea to its border. Beijing has constantly urged other powers not to push too hard on North Korea for fear of its collapse. To prevent refugees from entering China, it has built a barbed-wire fence along its 1,400 km border with North.[84]

Economic and Trade Relations: China is now the North's largest trading partner accounting for 85 percent of its foreign trade that amounted to $ 6.86 billion in 2014, up from only $ 490 million in 2000. North Korea's exports to China have been mostly coal and minerals, but these have been reduced because of the sanctions that the UN Security Council has placed on North Korea's exports and China's own sanctions.

But the relationship between Beijing and Pyongyang began to change after the North's first nuclear test in October 2006 when Beijing supported the UN Security Council Resolutions that imposed an increasingly severe regime of sanctions on North Korea. But China agreed to support these resolutions only after the tough sanctions on food and fuel imports by North Korea were removed. With the first resolution Beijing signaled a change in its attitude towards Pyongyang from support to punishment and has supported every subsequent resolution that sanctioned North Korea, but has had trouble enforcing them. Following the North's third nuclear weapon test in February 2013, Beijing summoned the North Korean ambassador in Beijing, imposed its own sanctions on the North, reduced its energy supplies and called for new denuclearization talks[85]

After the Chinese Foreign Minister Li Zhaoxing arrived late to a meeting during the 2005 ASEAN conference, he told the US Secretary of State Condoleezza Rice that when he tried to bring the

North Koreans into the meeting, he was chewed out by a North Korean political commissar, and said he "had never been talked to in that way.[86]

After North Korea's fifth test in September 2016, China and the United States jointly drafted UNSC Resolution 2321 which further tightened sanctions on Pyongyang including restrictions on its coal exports and on dual use items that could be used in North Korea's missile and nuclear weapons programs. In January 2017, Beijing issued a list of dual use items that it would not export to North Korea. Then after North Korea's missile test in February 2017, China terminated its purchase of coal from North Korea for the remainder of 2017 and after North Korea's sixth nuclear test on September 3, 2017. China supported UNSC Resolution 2375 that reduced North Korean fuel oil and energy imports by thirty percent, banned North Korea from exporting textile, and banned the renewal of contracts for North Korean workers abroad.

As the 105th anniversary of Kim Il-sung's birth on April 15, 2017 approached, satellite imagery of North Korea's nuclear test site at Punggye-ri showed that Pyongyang was preparing for a sixth nuclear weapons test. Beijing issued a warning to Pyongyang in the Global Times, an outlet of the Chinese Communist Party, "that another nuclear weapons test would take relations beyond the point of no return." On September 3, 2017, North Korea conducted its sixth nuclear weapon test that had a yield of between 75 and 100 kilotons, five times larger than its previous test, and may have been as large as 250 kt indicating that North Korea has mastered the technology of a boosted nuclear weapon or even for a true thermonuclear weapon.

China's dilemma with respect to Pyongyang is how much pressure it can put on Pyongyang: too much pressure could further alienate Kim Jong-un to act to harm China's strategic position in North East Asia and could even cause a collapse of the Pyongyang regime. China's dilemma is likely to become more intense as Pyongyang continues to pursue its nuclear weapons and missile programs. The Global Times editorial cited above remarked that "China had very little influence over present situation."[87]

And at a meeting of the Munich Security Conference Core Group in Beijing in November 2016, Chinese officials delivered a clear and unambiguous message that Beijing will not take any steps against Pyongyang that might increase the chance of a confrontation with it or encourage a regime change there. Beijing appears to value stability on the Korean Peninsula more than it fears the prospect that North Korea will become a full fledged nuclear power.[88] Indeed, a nuclear armed North Korea is a further deterrent to a South Korean attack that could bring US troops to China's border.

Recently Beijing appears to have become exasperated with its inability to influence Pyongyang's behavior regarding its nuclear weapons and missile programs. Following up on President Donald Trump's statement as a candidate that he would be willing to sit down with Kim Jong-un, share a hamburger and strike a deal with him, China's officials have encouraged Mr. Trump to seize the chance for a new chapter in dealing with North Korea. Lu Chao, director of the Border Study Institute at the Liaoning Academy of Social Studies in Shenyang, China remarked, "We all think that the Trump administration should talk directly with North Korea. That would be the best approach to crack this problem." Cheng Xiaohe at the Rennin University in Beijing said, "China wants America to talk directly with North Korea because it believes the North Korea nuclear problem was actually caused by the Cold War and Pyongyang fears of an American invasion. Therefore, the blame falls squarely in the United States, and all the negotiations should be about the United States talking to North Korea." Only after the United States has demonstrated a good faith effort to negotiate a deal with Pyongyang would Beijing be willing to engage Pyongyang to abandon its nuclear weapons and missile programs.[89]

The China-North Korea Security Relationship: In 1961 China and North Korea signed the Treaty of Friendship, Cooperation and Mutual Assistance, which Article II states, "The Contracting Parties undertake jointly to adopt all measures to prevent aggression against either of the Contracting Parties by any state. In the event of one of the Contracting Parties being subjected to the armed attack by any state or by several states jointly and thus being involved in a state of war, the other Contracting Party shall immediately render military and other assistance by all means at its disposal." The treaty was renewed in 1981 and again in 2001 and runs until 2021. On May 3, 2017, the Global Times ran an editorial that stated, North Korea's pursuit of nuclear technology has impaired its own security as well as the regions, and has also jeopardized China's national security. This has violated the principles of the treaty. The treaty firmly opposes aggression. But North Korea insists on developing nuclear weapons and conducting missile launches in violation of UN Security Council resolutions, which increases the risk of military clashes with the US. The situation has changed a lot compared with that of 2001 when the treaty was renewed. . . . North Korea must give up its nuclear weapons. . . . China will not allow its northeastern region to be contaminated by North Korea's nuclear activities. Nor will it allow changes in the peninsula through non-peaceful means. China has not imposed full scale sanctions on any country and the Chinese people have stayed away from war for years. The world has seen China's strength gaining momentum. China respects all countries but no country should underestimate China's determination.[90]

Several observers, including Bonnie Glazer of the Center for International and Strategic Studies in Washington, Zhang Baohui of Hong Hong's Lingnan University, Cai Jian of Fudan University in Shanghai and Anthony Wong Dong in Macau have interpreted the editorial as meaning that China will not assist North Korea not only if it initiates a war, but also if it is attacked. However the editorial may only be a threat to Pyongyang, and even if Pyongyang initiated a war, Beijing would very likely pursue its primary interest of preventing the fall of the Pyongyang regime and would come to its aid.

The Seoul-Beijing Relationship

China is South Korea's largest trading partner; in 2015 their trade amounted to $ 46.5 billion. On the other hand, Seoul is dependent on the United States for its security. Too close a relationship with the United States could risk damaging its economic relations with China, especially since the balance of power in the in the Western Pacific region is now shifting more and more in China's favor and against that of the United States, and as it does South Korea is likely to lose some of its independence and fall more and more into China's orbit.

After North Korea's fourth nuclear test in January 2016, South Korea's President Park Geun-hye tried to telephone China's President Xi Jinping, but her calls were not returned, and in the following days she decided to accept the US offer to deploy the THAAD missile defense system in South Korea. The Chinese response was quick and unforgiving: its ambassador to Seoul responded by saying that the THAAD in South Korea would, "destroy Sino-South Korean relations in a instant," and China's Foreign Minister Yang Yi said that Seoul's decision to deploy the THAAD undermined the mutual trust between South Korea and China. China claimed that the THAAD radar could monitor Chinese air space and hence was a US intelligence threat to China. China has also responded with some minor impositions on South Korea: It has forbidden the import of some luxury goods from South Korea; South Korean performers were forbidden from starring in Chinese performances; Beijing has instructed its travel agents to reduce the number of its tourists to South Korea by twenty percent; Beijing has removed the thirty kilogram duty free baggage on South Koreans entering China; and, it has cancelled charter flights from South Korea.

The United States South Korea Relationship

The United States and South Korea have a mutual defense treaty dating from 1954 that places South Korea under the US nuclear umbrella whereby the United States is obligated to come to South Korea's defense, including the use its nuclear weapons if South Korea suffers an attack. But North Korea's potential development of a capability to mount a nuclear attack against US territory has called this commitment into question in South Korea.

The credibility of the US commitments to-South Korea's defense has been demonstrated by the fact that 28,500 US troops are currently stationed in South Korea. After North Korea's January 2016 nuclear test, US B1B bombers flew from Guam few over the demilitarized zone and landed in South Korea. In April and March 2016, the United States and South Korea conducted the Key Resolve and Joint Eagle joint military exercises in which 15,000 US personnel participated. It was the largest joint exercise since 2010. The 2017 Foul Eagle joint exercise began in March 2017 in which 3,600 additional US troops joined those already stationed in South Korea.

After North Korea's fifth nuclear test on September 9, 2016, the United States and South Korea began planning to implement the US nuclear commitments to the defense of South Korea. On December 29, 2016 US and South Korean officials met in Washington and discussed the implementation of the US commitment to regularly deploy US strategic assets to defend South Korea against a nuclear or conventional attack by North Korea.

During a telephone conversation with South Korea's Acting President Hwang Kyo-ahn on January 28, 2017 President Trump reaffirmed "the US iron-clad commitment to defend South Korea, through the provision of extended deterrence, using the full range of military capabilities." On his visit to South Korea and Japan in February 2017 the US Secretary of Defense James Mattis also reaffirmed the US commitment to South Korea, "Any attack on the United States or our allies, will be defeated and any use of nuclear weapons would be met with a response that would be effective and overwhelming." In September 2017 the United States deployed the full complement of six THAAD TELs in South Korea.

The Unites States-North Korean Relationship

Ever since the division of the Korean Peninsula in 1945, the relationship between Pyongyang and Washington has been a hostile one. Yet on three occasions Washington and Pyongyang have negotiated agreements in which Pyongyang promised to give up its nuclear weapons and missile programs, only to violate them and see them dissolve. One of Pyongyang's major objectives is to be recognized as a great power and it believes the achievement of a peace treaty and diplomatic recognition by the United States would achieve this goal. Pyongyang also claims that Washington is preparing for a nuclear war with it and that it requires its nuclear weapons to deter such a war. It also claims that Washington does not recognize its legitimate defense requirements. Given the perceptions of both the United States and North Korea, the most likely prognosis of their relationship is a continuation of the current cold war between them

Chapter VIII

Moon Jae-in Faces North Korea

Moon Jae-in, a civil rights lawyer and the son of North Korean refuges who fled North Korea during the 1950-1953 Korean War, was elected president of South Korea on May 9, 2017, replacing the more conservative and scandal ridden Park Geun-hye. During his election campaign Moon promised to take a new approach in his dealing with Pyongyang that would emphasize engagement and dialogue which was also favored at the time by both China and the United States. He regarded the US approach of sanctions and pressure as ineffective and counterproductive; and that it was time for a different approach. But he also regarded South Korea's alliance with the United States as essential to his country's security. Moon also planned to review the decision to deploy the THAAD missile defense system that China regards as a threat and had placed some mild sanctions on South Korea for allowing its deployment. But after North Korea's sixth nuclear test in September 2017, Moon authorized the full deployment of the THAAD battery.

During his election campaign, Moon favored a new sunshine policy towards North Korea that included reopening the Kaesong Industrial Park that in 2013 employed 53,000 North Korean workers. Moon's strategy for engaging North Korea was focused

Figure 7 – Moon Jae-in

on economic engagement with Pyongyang.[92] After his election, Moon proposed that he and Kim Jong-un meet at Panmunjom and discuss family reunifications, curtailment of hostile activities along the DMZ and cooperation on the 2018 Winter Olympics to be held in South Korea, but Pyongyang's only response to Moon's overtures was a series of missile tests including two that Pyongyang called an ICBM and the September 3, 2017 large nuclear weapons test. These actions seemed to indicate that Pyongyang had rejected Moon's overtures to which Moon responded by saying, "The reality is that there is a high probability of a military conflict at the NLL (Northern Limit Line) and the DMZ."[93] Moon then recognized that Pyongyang poses an existential threat to his country.

Presidents Moon and Trump met in Washington on June 29 and 30, 2017 and agreed that Pyongyang must be dealt with a "stern response" to its provocations, and Moon promised to coordinate closely with Trump as he looks to intensify economic and diplomatic pressure on North Korea. Moon said that he and

Trump agreed to strengthen their deterrence and coordinate on their North Korean policy, employing both sanctions and dialogue "in a phased and comprehensive approach, [and] that denuclearization of the peninsula must be resolved without fail. North Korea should by no means underestimate the firm commitment by South Korea and the United States in this regard."[94]

After North Korea's presumed ICBM test on July 29, 2017, President Moon approached Washington to allow his country to develop more capable ballistic missile then are permitted under a 2012 agreement with the United States that limited South Korean missiles to a range of 800 km and a payload of 500 kg. Seoul wants to increase the payload limit to 1,000 kg. In a telephone conservation between the national security advisors of both countries, the US National Security Advisor Gen. H.R. McMaster agreed that South Korea would be allowed to develop new missiles with the increased payloads. President Moon also authorized the full deployment of the THAAD battery consisting of six transporter launchers, each with eight launch tubes.[95]

After North Korea's sixth nuclear test on September 3, 2017, South Korea's conservative Saenuri Party leaders began pushing for South Korea to develop its own nuclear weapons. In a recent poll, sixty percent of South Koreans agreed that their country should have its own nuclear weapons. But other lawmakers called for the redeployment of US tactical nuclear weapons in South Korea. South Korea's Defense Minister, Song Young-moo on September 4, 2017 said, "The redeployment of tactical nuclear weapons [in South Korea} is an alternative worth a full review," and he and US Secretary of Defense James Mattis discussed the matter during a meeting in Washington. Later, however, President Moon's office said that it was not considering redeploying tactical nuclear weapons nor the development of a South Korean nuclear weapon, "Our government's firm stance on a nuclear free peninsula remains unchanged."[96] Later Air Force General John

Hyten, chief of the US Strategic Command called the phrase "tactical nuclear weapons" a misnomer and "actually a very dangerous term because there are significant consequences to using nuclear weapons in any format . . . To call it a tactical weapon brings into the possibility that there could be a nuclear weapon employed on a battlefield for a tactical effect. It is not a tactical effect and if somebody employs what is a non-strategic or tactical nuclear weapon, the United States will respond strategically, not tactically, because they have crossed a line, a line that has not been crossed since 1945." As an alternative to South Korea developing its own nuclear weapons or redeploying US tactical nuclear weapons, the South Korean Defense Minister Song asked the US Secretary of Defense Mattis that US strategic assets such as US aircraft carriers, nuclear submarines and B-52 bombers be sent to South Korea more regularly.[97]

From the US perspective, the last thing that it would want is for South Korea to acquire its own nuclear weapons and abrogate its commitments under the Nuclear Nonproliferation Treaty. The United States is committed to the nuclear defense of South Korea to prevent it from becoming another nuclear weapons state.

Chapter IX

The North Korean Conundrum

Kim Jong-un's primary strategic objectives are first, the survival of the North Korean state, and second, the reunification of the Korean Peninsula under Pyongyang's rule. Kim regards the United States as the primary existential threat to North Korea. He claims that the tri-annual joint military exercises by the United States and South Korea, the 28,500 US troops stationed in South Korea, the frequent US BlB bomber over flights of the DMZ and their landings in South Korea and the deployment of US naval assets off the Korean coast are preparations for an invasion of his country and for nuclear war. To deter a joint United States and South Korean invasion of his country the Kim dynasty, beginning with his grandfather, have acquired an arsenal of powerful nuclear weapons and long range ballistic missiles capable of reaching deep into the continental United States. Kim knows, or should know, that the US nuclear capabilities overwhelm his own, and that his first use of nuclear weapons would bring an overwhelming, devastating response that would destroy his country .But he regards his own nuclear weapons as a deterrent of a US attack.

There are three possible outcomes to the current situation regarding North Korea: war; a negotiated solution in which North Korea would eliminate its nuclear weapons and ballistic missile programs; and a continuation of the status quo.

War is Unlikely but a Possibility

North Korea has threatened to attack both South Korea and the United States, and has accused both countries of plotting a nuclear war against it. A state of war technically exists between North Korea and the United States and South Korea because a peace treaty between the belligerents was never consummated after the Korean War.

A war on the Korean Peninsula would be catastrophe for all the parties involved. As the United States fulfilled its defense commitments to South Korea, it would most likely draw China into the war because China would not want the Pyongyang regime to fall, thus putting China and the United States on opposite sides of the conflict fighting one another. If North Korea felt that it was losing the war, it would likely use its nuclear weapons, and the United States would be obliged to respond with its nuclear weapons. The results would be millions of fatalities. During the initial phase of the war North Korea would use its missiles and heavy artillery that it has already deployed just north of the DMZ against South Korea killing hundreds of thousands of non-combatants in the Seoul metropolitan area. Even a conventional non-nuclear war would result in millions of casualties, and such a war could likely esculate into a nuclear war Over three million people lost their lives during the 1950-1953 Korean War. Thus all the parties are theoretically deterred from initiating even a conventional war because situation of mutual assured destruction (MAD) exists.

Nevertheless, a war could occur because of miscalculation. Even though China has said that it would not aid North Korea if it initiated a war, Pyongyang may not believe China and think that China would come to its aid to prevent the Pyongyang regime from collapsing. Pyongyang may further believe that it and China could defeat South Korea and the United States, or even that the

United States would not fulfill its commitments to South Korea, especially since North Korea possess nuclear weapons that could hit the continental United States and deter the United States from fulfilling its defense commitments to South Korea. (In 1941 Japan believed that the United States would not respond to its attack on Pearl Harbor, and if it did, Japan could defeat the crippled US Navy.

There is also the possibility that the leader in Pyongyang would have a death wish and would want to take the rest of the world down with him. Kim Il-sung once asked his son, Kim Jong-il what he would do if North Korea was losing a war, Kim Jong-il replied that he would destroy the world if North Korea as loosing a war because the world cannot exist without North Korea.)

Negotiated Outcome Is Unlikely

The most desirable outcome, but probably the least likely, is a negotiated one in which North Korea would agree to give up its nuclear weapons and ballistic missiles. But we've been down this road three times already and each time Pyongyang has violated the agreement causing them all to collapse.

Recently, in 2013, China tried to restart the Six Party Talks that were terminated in 2009 after North Korea conducted its first nuclear weapons test, but Pyongyang refused to participate. Kim Jong-il regards his nuclkear weapons as essential top his country's survival and is very unlikely to ever agree to relinquish them..

The only possibility of getting Pyongyang back to the negotiating table would be for China to slowly reduce the food and fuel oil that China supplies to North Korea until Pyongyang feels enough pain that it agrees to return to the negotiations, but this would be no guarantee of an agreement; and China seems unwilling to put enough pressure on Pyongyang to force it back to the negotiating table. Furthermore, North Korea probably can earn enough on its sales on the black market to make up for some of what China would not supply.

Pyongyang's interest in a peace treaty would be that it would include provisions for the removal of US troops from South Korea, but it is unlikely that Pyongyang would accept the quid pro quo that it eliminate its nuclear weapons and missile programs. Pyongyang could agree to another round of talks only for the sake of talks as it has done before because engaging in talks with the United States and China gives it the aura of being a significant power.

Even if Pyongyang agreed to another round of talks only for the sake of talks as it has done before because engaging in talks with the United States and China gives it the aura of being a significant power, and then it would either refuse to consummate an agreement or violate the agreement after it is signed, as it has done before.

Nevertheless, there are those who advocate renewed negotiations and if Pyongyang were to accept the offer, the opportunity should certainly be pursued, but with low expectations of a favorable outcome.

The Status Quo Has Its Dangers

The most likely outcome is a continuation of the cold war status quo in which all parties are deterred from war by the threat of mutual assured destruction (MAD). But unlike the situation prevailed during the Cold War between the West and the Soviet Union, the status quo is fraught with the dangers discussed above. In the long run, the status quo would be an unstable situation in which Pyongyang, counting on Beijing's support could launch an attack on South Korea.

Another possibility is a war could break out because of the vindictiveness and hostile dialogue between the leaders in Washington and Pyongyang.

Perhaps some future leader would want to bring North Korea into the modern world and develop its economy as Deng Xiaoping in China, or Mikhail Gorbachev did in the Soviet Union. But that day is far in the future.

End Notes

1. Don Oberdorfer and Robert Carlin, The Two Koreas: A Contemporary History, Revised and Updated, 3rd ed., New York 2014, Basic Books, an imprint of Perscus Books LLC, a subsidiary of Hachette Book Group Inc., p. xii

2. Nicole Gaouette, "North Korea at the UN: US faces consequences beyond imagination," CNN, September 23, 2016, www.cnn.com/2016/09/22/politics/north-korea-nu-ascan/.

3. Jun Il Bye, "US nuclear weapons may be deployed in South Korea," Korean Times, October21, 2016, www.korea\ntimes.com.kr//www/news/nation2016//10/116_216816.html.

4. "US to regularly deploy strategic weapons in South Korea Officials say," TV Press, December 21, 2016, www.presstv.comDetail/2016/12/21/5008-48/us-strategic-weaponn-south-korea.

5. "Readout of President's Call with South Korea Acting President President Hwang Kyu-han," Office of the Press Secretary, The White House, January 29, 2017.

6. "Mattis Threatens North Korea Deploying Nuks Means War,". TRU, February 3, 2017, www.trunews.com/article/mattis-threatens-north-korea-deploying-nuks-means -war.

7. Photo by the Korean Central News Agency

8. Photo by the Korean Central News Agency, March 15, 2016

9. Photo by the Korean Cent`ral News Agency.

10. Ibid.

11. Nuclear Threat Initiative, "Missiles," July 2017. www.nti.org/Learn/countries/north-korea//delivery-systems/

12. Oberdorfer and Carlin 2014, loc. 3cit. n.1, p. 5.

13. Quoted in ibid, p. 14.

14. Ibid, p. 15.

15. Ibid, p. 7

16. Ibid.

17. Ibid, p.8

18. Charles K. Armstrong, "The Destruction and Reconstruction of North

19. H.W. Brands, The General and the President: MacArthur and Truman At The Brink of Nuclear War, New York, Doubleday 2015, eboo   k edition, p 80.

20. Ibid, p. 220

21. Ibid. p.222

22. V. Hasbrouck, "Memo to File, November 7, 1951," G-3 Operations file box 38A, Library of Congress.

23. Army Chief of Staff, "Memo to file, November 20, 1951," G-3 Operations file box 38A, Library of Congress.

24. Lee Jae-Bong, "US Deployment of Nuclear Weapons in 1950s South Korea and North Korea's Nuclear Deployment: Towards Denuclearization of the Korean Peninsula," The Asia-Pacific Journal, Vol. 7, issue 8 (February 2008)

25. Ibid.

26. Ibid.

27. A History of U.S. Nuclear Weapons in South Korea, The Nuclear Information Project, September 28, 2005, www.nucstrat.com/korea/koreahistory.htm

28. "U.S. to Pull Nuclear Arms from Korea," The Washington Post, October 19, 1991.

29. Siegfried Hecker, "What to Make of North Korea's Lateest Nuclear Test: An Interview with Siegfried Hecker," 38North, September 30, 2016, 38north.org/201609/shocker091216.

30. 38 NORTH, "Sixth Nuclear Test Detected at Punggye-ri, Decl;ared to be a Hydrogen Bomb," www.38north.org/ 2017/09/nuke0900317.

31. Elisabeth Eaves, "North Korea nuclear test shows steady advance: interview with Siefried Hecker," Bulletin of Atomic Scientists, http://the bulletin.org/north-korean-nuclear-test-shows-steady-advance-interview-with-siegfried-hecker.

32. Ibid.

33. Nuclear Threat Initiative, North Korea's Strategic Threat: Overview: Missile, July, 2017, www.nti.org/learn/Countries/ north-korea/delivery-systms/

34. Ibid.

35. Ibid.
36. Ibid.
37. William J. Broad and David E, Sanger, "The Rare, Potent Fuel; Powering North Korea's Weapons," The New York Times, September 17, 2017.
38. Operational Capability, 38North, May 24, 2017, www.38morth.org2017/05jsschilling052017.
39. John Schilling, "What Next for North Korea's ICBM?" 38North, August 1, 2017, www.38north.org/2017/08/jschilling080117/
40. Theodore Postal, Markus Schiller and Robert Schneider, "North Korea's 'not quite' ICBM can't hit lower 48," Bulletin of Atomic Scientists, August 11, 2017, thebullitn.org/north-korea%E2^%80%99s%-%E2%80%9Cnot-quite%E2%80%9D-icbm
41. Ibid.
42. David E. Sanger and William J. Broad, "Trump Inherits a Secret Cyberwar Against North Korean Missiles," The New York Times, March 5, 2017.
43. "South Korea Nuclear Developments and Strategic Decision Making," National Foreign Assessment Center, Central Intelligence Agency, June 1978, www.natulis.org/wp-content/uploads/2011/09/cia_rok_nuclear_decisionmaking.pd
44. Oberdorfer and Carlin 2014, loc. cit., n.1, p.56.
45. Ibid. p. 58.
46. Ibid.
47. Martin Facker and Choe San-hun, "South Korea Flirts with Nuclear Ideas as North Blusters," New York Times, March 10, 2013.
48. Robert Einhorn and Duyeon Kim, "Will South Korea Go Nuclear?"hppt://the.bulliten.org/will-south-korea-go-nuclear977/ (This paper is the result of interviews that Einhorn and Kim conducted in South Korea in March and April 2016.)
49. "60% of S. Koreans Support Nuclear Armament, Poll," The Korean Times, September 23, 2014, http://www.koreatimes.co.kr/www/news/nation/2016/09/205_214598.html
50. This section draws on material from Oberdorfer and Calin 20`4, loc. Cit., n. 1, pp. 209-224.

51. US-DPRK Agreed Framework, Inventory of Internatrional Nonproliferation Organizations and Regimes Center for Nonproliferation Studies
52. Oberdorfer and Calin 2014, loc. cit., n. 1, p. 3678.
53. Condoleezza Rice, No Higher Honor: A Memoir of My Years in Washington, New York, 2011, Crown Publishing Group, p. 248f
54. Ibid, p. 516.
55. Ibid, p. 572.
56. Andrew Quinn, "Insight: Obama's North Korean leap of faith falls short," Reuters, March 30, 2012, www.reuters.com/articles/us-korea-north-usa-leap-idUSBBRE82T06T20120330.
57. Ankit Pand, "A Great Leap Forward to Nowhere: Remembering tj US-North Korea 'Leap Day' Deal," The Diplomat, February 29, 2016, hppt://thediplomat.com/2016/02/a-great-leap-forward-to-nowhere-rembering-the-us-north-korea-
58. Carol Morello, Michelle Yo Hee Lee,and Emily Rauhela, " U.N. agrees to toughest-ever sanctions against North Korea," The Washington Post, September 11, 2017
59. Report of the Panel of Experts established pursuant to resolution 1874, UN Security Council Document 2017/150, February 27, 2017
60. Coco Liu, "Sanctions are Fine, But What About The Chionese Who Depend On Trade With North Korea?" South China Post, July 9, 2017 www.scmp.com/week-asia/business/article/2101743/sanctions-are-fine-but-what-about-tghe-chinese-who-depen-on-trade-with-north-korea.
61. Scott Snyder, "How North Korea Evades UN Sanctions Through Inter-national Front Compnies," Forbes, March 3, 2017, www.forbes.com/ sites/scottsnyder2017/03/03/how-north-korea-evades-sanctions
62. Jane Perlez, Yufan Huang and Paul Mozur, "How North Korea Managed to Defy Years of Sanctions," The New York Times, May 12, 2017.
63. David Thompson, Risky Business, C4ADS, 2017
64. Snyder 2017, loc. cit., n.55.
65. John King Fairbank, The United States and China, Cambridge MA, Harvard University Press, 1983, p. 49.
66. Ibid, p. 115f.

67. James Leung, "Xi's Corruption Crackdown," Foreign Affairs, May/June, 2015, pp. 32-38.

68. Joby Warrick, "How Russia quietly undercuts sanctions intended to stop North Korea's nuclear program," The Washington Post, September 11, 2017.

69. David S. Cohen, "One powerful weapon to use against North Korea, The Washington Post, April 21, 2017.

70. David Nakamura and Greg Jaffe, "US announces sanctions on Chinese bank, arms-sales package for Taiwan," The Washington Post, June 29, 2017

71. Grace Lee, "The Political Philosophy of Juche," The Stanford Journal of East Asian Affairs, v.3, n. 1 (Spring 2003), pp. 103-1112

72. Oberdorfer and Carlin 2014, loc. cit., n. 1, p15f.

73. Ibid, p. 337.

74. Lee 2003, loc. cit., n. 64

75. Ibid.

76. Ibid.

77. Ibid.

78. Park Young Ho, "South and North Korea's Views on the Unification of the Korean Peninsula and Inter-Korean Relations," Presented at the KRIS-Brookings Joint Conference on Security and Diplomatic Cooperation between ROK and US for the Unification of the Korean Peninsula, January 21, 2014.

79. Ibid.

80. Ibid.

81. Einhorn and Kim 2016, loc. citr., n. 48.

82. Ibid.

83. Ibid.

84. Albert 2016, loc. cit., n. 72.

85. China gives details of items banned for export to North Korea," www.reuters.com/article/us-china-northkorea-nuclear-idUSKBN159160?utm_source..., Jamuary 26,2017.

86. Rice , loc. cit., n. 53, p. 709.

87. Wang Tianmi and Liu Xin, "China may reconsider NK policies involving Sino-USties," Global Times. April 18m 2017, www.g;obltimes.cn/content/1042932.dhtml.

88. Jane Perlez, Choe Sabg-hun and Motoko Rich, "Trump's Muted Tone on North Korea Gives Hopes for Nuclear Talks," The New York Times, February 14, 2017

89. Ibid.

90. Jesse Johnson, "For North Korea and China, defense pact proves a complicated document," The Japanese Times, May 10, 2017,

91. Jesse Johnson, North Korea and China, defense pact proves a complicated document," The Japanese Times, May 10, 2017

92. "Advisory panel stresses Moon's focus on inter-Korean economic cooperation," Yonhap News, May 26, 2017, hppt://english.yonhapnews.co.kr/northkorea.2017/2-17/05/26/0401000000AEN2017052600890

93. "S. Korea's Moon says high possibility of conflict with North Korea as missile crisis builds," www.cnbc.com/2017/05/17/sout-koreas-moon-jac-in-says-high-possibility-of-conflict/

94. Mathew Pennington, "Trump ops trade tensions with S. Korea in welcoming new leader," The Washington Post, June 30, 2017.

95. Hoe Sang-hun and David Sanger, North Korea's Test, South Korea Pushes to Build UP Its Own Missiles, The Ne w York Times, July 29, 2017.

96. Ryan PPrickrell, "South Korea Debates Bringing Tactical Nukes Back As North Korean Bombs Get Bigger," $The Daily Caller, September 11, 2017, http://dailycaller.com/2017/09/11/south-korea-debates-bringing-tactical-nukes-back-as-north-korean-bombs-get-bigger/

97. Don Lamothe, "Pentagon chief says he was asked about reintroducing tactical nuclear weapons in South Korea," The Washington Post, September 18, 2017

About the Author

George R. Pitman is retired from the US Arms Control and Disarmment Agency and from the US Department of State. He holds a PhD in physics and has studied international relations at UCLA. He is the author of Why War: An Inquiry into the Genetic and Social Sources of Human Warfare, Neither War nor Peace: A History of the Cold War and Strategic Arms Control From 1946 to 1973 and Arms Races and Sable Deterrence.

www.ingramcontent.com/pod-product-compliance
Lightning Source LLC
Chambersburg PA
CBHW062011280526
45787CB00005B/2057